Interact

Youth Work

Practice

Number 1 in a series of
youth work resources

Mark A. Krueger

CWLA Press • Washington, DC

CWLA Press is an imprint of the Child Welfare League of America. The Child Welfare League of America (CWLA) is a privately supported, non-profit, membership-based organization committed to preserving, protecting, and promoting the well-being of all children and their families. Believing that children are our most valuable resource, CWLA, through its membership, advocates for high standards, sound public policies, and quality services for children in need and their families.

CHILD WELFARE LEAGUE OF AMERICA, INC.
440 First Street, NW, Third Floor, Washington, DC 20001-2085
E-mail: books@cwla.org

CURRENT PRINTING (last digit)
10 9 8 7 6 5 4 3 2 1

Cover design by Veronica J. Morrison
Author photo by Bill Herrick

Printed in the United States of America

ISBN # 0–87868-707-6

Library of Congress Cataloging-in-Publication Data
Krueger, Mark A.
    Interactive youth work practice /   Mark Krueger.
        p.   cm.
    Includes bibliographical references.
    ISBN 0-87869-707-6 (alk. paper)
    1. Social work with youth.   2. Interpersonal relations.
    I. Title.
    HV 1421.K78   1998   98-39362
    362.7'083--dc21   CIP

Contents

Foreword

The 1990s have presented tremendous challenges to young people and to the adults who work with them. Government officials, policymakers, and community members express ongoing concern about societal issues that have a negative impact on youth, such as violence, poverty, and early parenthood. While youth work has moved steadily toward solid strengths-based practice, recent legal and social responses to concerns about young people have been largely punitive and rely on increased control of and coercive adult intervention in youth behavior. In this climate, youth workers must not only help young people develop skills and competencies, but also partner with them to advocate effectively for a more balanced and positive view of youth.

The Child Welfare League of America has a long history of producing and disseminating resources that support best practice and innovation in child welfare and related disciplines. *Youth Work Resources* is a series of books designed to access the knowledge and experience of youth workers who play a critical role in providing services to youth in child welfare and other settings.

While we are still in the process of defining youth work as a profession, we have a clear understanding of what youth workers do. Wherever youth workers are employed or volunteer, they promote the positive development of young people. Across the nation every day, in residential facilities, community centers, schools, YMCAs, churches, shelters, and streets, youth workers put all of their skills and much of their hearts into helping young people achieve their goals, dreams, and safe passages into adulthood.

In *Interactive Youth Work Practice*, the first book in the *Youth Work Resources* series, Mark Krueger addresses the need for youth workers to be in the world with youth ... bring[ing] themselves, their skills, and their knowledge to the moment and [being] sensitive to the needs of the youth and the contexts within which their interactions occur. They are musicians and technicians, friends and adults in charge, masters of the situation, and fellow travelers on a journey of discovery and growth.

Interactive Youth Work Practice emphasizes youth work as a way of being with young people, as well as a set of behaviors and skills. Krueger draws on his many years of observation and experience as a youth worker to create a working and learning tool for building positive, productive relationships with young people.

Future publications in the *Youth Work Resources* series will focus on such topics as independent living services, positive youth development, and adventure programs. We hope that these books contribute to the growing body of knowledge about what works best to promote the development of young people, and that they validate the primary role of the direct service youth worker in creating better futures for our youth.

Robin Nixon
Director, Youth Services
Child Welfare League of America

Introduction

In a park across the street from the youth center, a female worker and a teenage boy are playing catch. A male worker and girl are sitting on a park bench drawing. As a boy and a girl walk across the street to the park, the worker at the park bench invites them over.

This book examines an interactive approach to youth work practice. The major thesis is that youth develop in moments and interactions, such as those described above, and that these moments and interactions are enhanced when workers have the capacity to guide, teach, learn, and be *with* youth in a manner that is sensitive to youth's developmental capacities and readiness for growth, and to the multiple contexts within which interactions take place [Baizerman 1996; Bruner 1990; Fewster 1990; Maier 1987; NACCYCEP 1995].

I designed the five essays for reflection and discussion. The first essay provides definitions of youth development and youth work. Context and understanding, essential elements in interacting with youth, are explored in the second and third essays.

The fourth essay defines four themes—presence, meaning, rhythm, and atmosphere—in interactions. In the fifth essay, the themes are discussed, along with context and understanding, as a guide for daily interactions. At the end, I have provided practice examples and a curriculum outline for people who wish to teach and learn the interactive approach in university classrooms or inservice training sessions.

In preparing to read the book, it might be helpful to think of youth work as a shared journey: workers and youths going through the day, learning and growing together.

Essay One
Interactive Youth Development and Youth Work

This essay provides definitions of interactive youth development and youth work for discussion. The purpose is to introduce concepts and themes that will be woven throughout the book.

Youth Development

Think of a moment of your youth. Try to remember who was there and what you were doing. Or maybe you were alone, doing something or nothing by yourself. Maybe you sense the sounds and smells of the moment. You feel a certain way: happy, sad, anxious, exuberant, relaxed, connected, alienated, etc. This moment, along with thousands of other moments, is part of your story, a story that guides your actions and contributes to the feelings you have about yourself and others. You see and experience the world through a lens that has been crafted by these moments—a changing narrative that includes many instances of joy, happiness, struggle, sadness, and discovery.

Similarly, in the interactive approach, youth are viewed as unique developing beings, who build and shape themselves into the world through unique cultural and familial experiences [Bruner 1990; Fewster 1990; Maier 1987; Vygotsky 1978]. As they interact, they change people and environ-

1

ments, and people and environments change them. This ongoing process of interaction creates their evolving story and further determines how they see, sense, and experience the world.

Adolescence, from this perspective, is a journey filled with paradox, struggle, and challenge. Youth search for their uniqueness within the bounds of their desire to be accepted; test the elasticity of their desire to be part of and separate from their parents, friends, and heroes; perform for real and imaginary audiences; and rebel against perceived and real authority amidst the groans and moans of their rapidly changing bodies, minds, and sexual feelings.

The journey through adolescence is enhanced in moments of connection:

A youth enters a neighborhood center for the first time. The worker welcomes him at the door, walks with him through the halls and activity areas, pointing out and describing the range of activities. The worker is present in the moment. She listens to the boy, invites questions, and answers with a genuine interest.

A boy and a girl walk through a park. "Did you ever think there are no words for feelings?" the boy asks.

"Yes, it's hard sometimes to describe how you feel. That's why I like to dance and run."

She runs ahead. He follows.

A worker walks into a youth's room at the group home, raises the shade, leans over the youth who is still in bed sleeping, gently shakes his shoulder, and calmly says, "Good morning."

Discovery fuels the journey [Vygotsky 1978]. Youth are changed and strengthened by new insights, insights that they discover about themselves and the world around them.

A youth walks with a worker in silence along a city street, then the youth says, "I think I get sad because my dad isn't around more."

A group of youth are working together on a set for their upcoming play. In front of them are the blueprints one youth prepared. One girl paces off the distance between where a door and a table will be placed, says, "In order to move the way we want in this space, we're going to need more space between the door and the table."

A sense of purpose [Bruner 1990] and a sense of oneness with the task at hand [Cskszentmihaly 1990] also enhance the journey.

A worker and a youth rake leaves. They want to clear the lawn before the first snow-fall.

A group of youth are playing catch with a football, lost in the activity.

In summary, youth development is a process of connection, discovery, and purpose. A shared journey with workers and other youth. A series of moments of togetherness, new insight, and vocation [Baizerman 1997; Baizerman & Magnusen 1996]. We are here, you and I, and it is good to be here, learning, struggling, succeeding, and being together.

Youth Work

In this context of youth development, youth work is a process of self in action [Baizerman 1996; Fewster 1990; Garfat 1996; Krueger 1997]. Workers bring themselves and their knowledge of adolescent development to the moment and choose to act or not act with skill as indicated by need and circumstance. Like modern dancers, workers learn technique (how to move) and plan (orchestrate and choreograph); practice and learn new steps that can be applied to new situations (changing tempos); and try to move in synch with the rhythms of the day and youth's developmental readiness to grow.

Struggle, as well as joy, is part of the process. As workers and youth move in and out of sync, the focus is simultaneously on who these youth are, what they do (or don't do), how they do it, where they do it, who they do it with, and in what context they do it. Workers understand that the answers to the questions are constantly changing with variations in the music, or score of the game, or mood of the youth, or new experience.

In interactive youth work, the emphasis is on interaction and moments of being together, more than the input, output, or outcome. The way of being with rather than the way of doing it to.

It is worker as dancer, artist, technician, ball player, choreographer, fellow traveler, and friendly ear. Not workers who mechanically build trust and skills, but dancers who are in the world with youth and so disclose trust and learning as fundamental to being together [Baizerman 1997]. Workers who ask such questions as: Am I being real? Are my actions geared to the youth's developmental strengths, abilities, and readiness? Do I understand? Am I using my knowledge, experience, and skills in the proper context? Are we in sync and what is the tone or mood of the moment? Workers who act, or choose not to act, in a manner that enhances growth.

A worker comes into work and meets a group of youth in the recreation room at the neighborhood center. He tries to focus himself in the moment. In the back of his mind are several thoughts about the day's activities and each of the youth with whom he is about to interact. He has planned a series of activities. Smiling, he moves forward, stands in what he considers to be the most strategic place, smiles, asks, "So, how's it going?"

Thus, youth work from an interactive perspective is a way of *being* as well as a way of *behaving*. Workers try to be in the world with youth. They bring themselves, their skill, and their knowledge to the moment and are sensitive to the needs of the youth and the contexts within which their interactions occur. They are musicians and technicians, friends and adults in charge, masters of the situation, and fellow travelers on a journey of discovery and growth.

Interactive Youth Work and the Challenges, Struggles, and Activities of Adolescence

In a powerful video series, Sadie Benning portrays her journey through adolescence in Milwaukee [Benning 1994]. With vivid images, words, and music, she captures many of the central struggles and feeling states of being a teenager.

She is in her room. With a close-up of her face, she says, "I guess when you're alone you get to know yourself for you and not who you're with. And I like that."

She stands in front of an American flag in a blond wig, changing her expression to the music, and the paradoxes she sees in world. The values, violence, and materialism. She looks at photos of her childhood. Talks about her friends. Looks out into the street, questions where she belongs, slides a handwritten note in front of the camera, "I'm scared a lot."

The camera scans her room, the overhead light, a couch, the dresser. She slowly slides her comb down in front of the camera, shifts to a window fan. Street noise can be heard, music in the background.

"You know, I suppose it's not so incredible, not so amazing that I find myself sitting here next to you wanting to laugh. I must laugh at it. And it so happens that we are here, at this moment, in the middle of a crowded restaurant. (The camera scans the room.) I want badly to yell out, but I don't want to cause a commotion, tension makes me nervous. And we are all eating, 800 million other faces. All of us concerned about what concerns us, and we're talking and listening, exchanging glances, taking a drink, and me, I'm numb. I've got a headache. I can think of a million other places I'd rather be."

She gets close to, fights with a boy in her class. Leaves school, forms a peer group of girls who understand. Gets into a fight with the boy on the bus.

Looking into the camera, she says, "I picture my life before now. It was cool, and I'm starting to feel different now, even in this room with 800 million other faces."

She is going to Detroit and Hollywood with a friend. They don't get there. They get only as far as a parking lot. She creates Hollywood in her head, her own world of fantasy, a place she often retreats to. "It wasn't love, but it was something," she says.

She begins a segment, "You know, I've been waiting ..."

As Sadie and so many youth remind us, adolescence is a period in life when the quest to understand ourselves and others is enriched with new sexual feelings and ways of thinking, and confused by a world full of paradox and fears. It is also the time of moving from childhood to adulthood—a longing to return to simpler moments, while simultaneously wanting to be grown up. "I remember how proud I was of the life I brought into this world," Sadie says as she discusses the conflicts in her world and questions what her life will be like as an adult.

Interactive workers are in the world with youth. They model a sense of curiosity about life and serve as a sort of "human place" for youth to return when they feel lost (stretched too far away from who they sense they are), or afraid of what they think they are becoming. Youth come to them for advice, guidance, and reassurance, or to just be with them as they move through transitions and activities.

"What was it like the first time you had sex?" a teenage girl asks a male worker.

The worker thinks a moment. "I wasn't ready."

"Why do you say that?"

"I'm not sure. Maybe because, later, when I was more secure about myself, it seemed different."

A worker hangs with a group of youth. He has no plan, no goal other than to just be in the moment with youth with a sense of anticipation.

Three youth stand next to a worker at her easels. Out of the corners of their eyes they watch as the worker paints, the certainty of her strokes, her enthusiasm for what she is doing.

A worker is moving with a group of youth from the playground to the youth center. They have been playing basketball and will get a bite to eat. Before moving they stood on the edge of the court a moment, talked, and cooled down. The worker has positioned himself in the middle of their movement. As a couple of youth move further ahead, he says, "No need to rush. There will be plenty to eat." The youth in front slow down a little bit.

A group of youth and a worker are sitting in a circle talking about the upcoming week. "Here's what we got planned so far," the worker goes through the list. "Some of these activities and routines, of course, are required, I think we agree on that. But what else might we do?"

A worker is making a pizza with three youth. One youth is rolling the dough. The other making a sauce. The third youth is preparing several toppings with the worker. "I can't wait to see what this will taste like," the worker says.

"Yeah, I've never had black olives," says one of the youth.

"Let's try some provolone cheese instead of mozzarella," another youth says.

A youth enters a program. A worker extends his hand, welcomes the youth, gets an initial sense of the youth's boundaries. Over the next few steps, they feel each other out, sense the tempo of their ability and/or desire to share space and limits.

A worker holds a youth, restrains him from hurting himself. The youth screams and hollers obscenities, tries to bite and hit the worker. Slowly the struggle subsides. The worker feels the tension in the youth's muscles lessen and senses the youth's readiness to be released.

Standing over a youth in bed with the lights out, a worker thinks about the youth's day and previous experiences, bends over, gently brushes the youth's hair back, pulls the covers to her chin.

Three youth and a worker are running. The worker pulls back from the group a few paces, slides over and gets in the middle where he can be closer to one youth who seems to be tiring and getting frustrated.

"I'm angry at what you did, but I still care about you. What I'd like to discuss is how we can keep it from happening again," a worker says.

"I really enjoyed myself with you today, but now it is time to settle down for dinner," another worker says.

Summary

Youth develop in moments of connection, discovery, and purpose. Their journey through adolescence is filled with struggles, challenges, and new insights.

Youth work is a process where each moment and interaction has enormous potential. Competent youth workers bring themselves to the moment, act as indicated by opportunity and circumstance, and share the journey with youth. They use their self-awareness, skills, and relationships to help youth in their search for an identity, to belong and become independent, to develop healthy relationships with peers, to explore their expanding worlds, and to understand their sexual feelings. They try to guide youth through transitions, engage them in activities that build on opportunities and strengths, and search with them for boundaries that allow room for connections.

References & Recommended Readings

Baizerman, M. (1996). Can we get there from here: A response to Shealy. *Child & Youth Care Forum, 25*, 285-288.

Baizerman, M. (1997). The sources of our expertise: A response to Krueger. *Child and Youth Care Forum, 26*, 417-419.

Baizerman M., & Magnusen, D. (1996). *Vocation, calling, and response as grounds to method and skill.* Paper presented at International Conference on Residential Group Care, Glasgow, Scotland.

Benning, S. (1994). *Videos by Sadie Benning.* Chicago: Video Data Bank.

Bruner, J. (1990). *Acts of meaning.* Cambridge, MA: Harvard University Press

Childress, H. (1996). *Landscapes of betrayal, landscapes of joy: Curtisville in the lives of its teenagers.* Unpublished doctoral dissertation, University of Wisconsin-Milwaukee.

Cskszentmihaly, M. (1990). *Flow: The psychology of optimal experience.* New York: Harper and Row.

Fewster, G. (1990). *Being in child care: A journey into self.* New York: Haworth.

Garfat, T. (1996). *The effective child and youth care intervention: A phenomenolgical inquiry.* Unpublished doctoral dissertation, University of Victoria, British Columbia, Canada.

Krueger, M. (1997). A contribution to the dialogue about the soul of professional development. *Child and Youth Care Forum, 26,* 411-415.

Maier, H. (1987). *Developmental group care of children and youth.* New York: Haworth.

North American Consortium of Child and Youth Care Education Programs. (1995). Curriculum content for child and youth care practice: Recommendations of the task force of the North American Consortium of Child and Youth Care Education Programs. *Child and Youth Care Forum, 24,* 269-278.

Vygotsky, L. S. (1978). *Mind in society.* Cambridge, MA: Harvard University Press.

Essay Two
Context

> It is in recognition of the contexts of the moment in every-day life that the youth worker may be the strongest. [Baizerman 1993, p. 245]

Consider that you are a youth worker, an experienced street worker in a large city. You see four teenage boys you know hanging on a corner, about a block away. A teenage girl approaches from the opposite direction, has a few words with one of the boys. As you get closer, you can hear their conversation:

"Ho," the boy says.

"Pimp."

"Ho!"

"Pimp!"

"Bitch!"

"Fuck you!"

They move forward, then away, then back toward each other. You approach. In the back of your mind is the moment from your own youth and hundreds of moments before and after that have shaped your view of encounters on the street. As you move closer, you simultaneously consider a number of factors, such as whether this is a fight about to start or simply a way of challenging or testing one another, doing a sort of street dance. You try to see the world through their eyes, look for clues. What do their expressions, the tones of their voices, and the posture of their bodies tell you about whether you should intervene or stand by? How will the other people in the area, the traffic, the noise, your feelings of fear or anxiety, the youth's feelings, and their interpretations of what's going on, influence what you will do?

You decide to act or not act. You might just stand in certain place, silently, or make a comment to divert their attention, such as "Hey, what's going on?" or make a directive statement, such as, "All right, cool it!" depending on your assessment of the context in which you will interact with them.

As you act or don't act, you are sensitive to your demeanor, your sense of presence and the impression it conveys. Your tone of voice or silence is firm but friendly.

This is an example of youth work in context. You entered a situation with sensitivity to your own feelings and experiences, to the meaning that the interaction might have for youth, to the space in which they are interacting, their familiarity with one another, and a variety of other factors—and then chose to act or not act accordingly.

Understanding Context: A Few Examples

Several authors have provided insight into the meaning and effects of context [Arieli 1996; Baizerman 1996; Beker et al. 1972; Maier 1995; Redl & Wineman 1957]. Recently, Maier [1995] described and analyzed moments of participation, being with youth, anticipation, and interactions in several rich, descriptive narratives. His case examples and stories provide a sense of the spaces and circumstances in which workers and youth interact, struggle, and succeed.

Garfat [1995] examined interventions in detail from worker and youth perspectives. From his analysis, we get a greater understanding of how workers and youth "make meaning" of an intervention, how the contexts for an intervention are different for worker and youth, and how success is rooted in developing an understanding of these contexts.

Williams [1995] experienced transitions with youth and described how rhythm, mood, and atmosphere enhanced their movement from one phase of a program to another. His thesis provides insight for creating a climate of welcome and trust in the early phases of out-of-home care by understanding the contexts in which youth enter a program.

Childress [1996] spent time with youth on street corners, in parking lots, and at the beach, trying to understand why they "hung out" in these places. The results of his study shed light on how workers can be with and engage youth in creating spaces, places, and attitudes that promote growth. His work gives us a better sense of the contexts for feelings and attitudes such as joy and anticipation.

Richmond [1998] is currently using self-reflection, dialogue, interviews, and literature searches to study boundaries. What are boundaries? What are their roles? How does a worker learn boundaries? How much is internal? How much external? Are they firm, flexible? What is the story of boundaries in specific interactions? When is it okay to touch or not touch, tighten or loosen limits?

Fewster [1990] based his novel on a discussion between a supervisor and worker about a sexually abused girl, and explored in depth and with wonderful insight the processes of self-discovery and presence in child and youth care. We become engaged in the moments of the story and feel, learn, and sense how our experience influences how we are with youth.

Freeman [1993] and Baizerman [1993] discussed the importance of creating and adjusting to context, using as a focal point Freeman's story, "Jacob and the Preacher: A Conversation in Context." Their dialogue provides insight into how self-awareness, understanding, use of space and timing, tone, and mood come together in a counseling situation with a youth in a cafe.

Each of these studies emphasizes workers, youth, and the situations and spaces in which they interacted. Each author made efforts to get engaged in situations and to try to understand the meaning of what was occurring. They paid attention to tone, mood, time, place, perception, and circumstance. The authors tried to feel and sense the story of a moment and interaction and to understand it through the eyes of youth as it occurred.

Competence

Competence in interactive youth work practice includes the capacity to understand and be sensitive to contexts.

A worker decides the time is right to talk and listen. She has just finished jogging through the neighborhood with a 16-year-old boy, and they are sitting on a park bench. She senses that the boy is worried about a first date he has that evening. Earlier, he had been boastful with his peers. She begins with the question, "So, are you excited about your date tonight?" then focuses her attention on the youth while simultaneously paying attention to her presence in the moment. As he speaks, she listens with enthusiasm and sensitivity.

A worker knows that a youth is upset about something that went on at the youth's home—perhaps an argument between the youth's parents. The worry is evident in the youth's appearance and actions. But there are several other youth present and a cleaning chore to be completed. The worker considers pulling the youth aside, decides instead to wait. Perhaps the activity will get the youth's mind off home, then the worker will talk with the youth later when the other youth are engaged in another activity. Sensing the youth's need for assurance, the worker works next to this youth, hoping the youth will sense his concern as well as pleasure to be working alongside of him.

A worker enters a youth's house to have a discussion with his parents. As he walks through the door, he tries to be sensitive to the unique cultural context in which the youth's family lives. He realizes he is in their space and tries to acknowledge the rituals and traditions of their home life without making stereotypic judgments about what he sees, smells, hears, and senses.

The following are examples of how specific competencies for interactive youth work can be defined in context.

Listening. Workers know and are sensitive to when to listen and not to listen. They have the capacity to be present in the moment and are capable of giving the youth their undivided attention. While listening, they demonstrate such listening skills as maintaining eye contact and nodding their head in sync with the listening experience and meaning of the words expressed by youth. They create and/or adjust physical space (chairs, lights, noise levels) to accommodate listening. Through attitude and feedback, they also demonstrate the capacity to understand the meaning of youth's words and actions and the interrelatedness with preceding and following events.

Waking Youth Up. In waking a youth up, workers demonstrate sensitivity to the meaning of sleep and the transition from sleep to being awake. For example, a worker demonstrates when to raise or lower his or her voice and when to touch or not touch a youth in the morning. Workers also know when to turn on a light or raise a shade, as well as how much instruction to expect youth to follow. They foreshadow upcoming events and help youth with chores, such as finding their shoes and making their beds, with consideration to each youth's developmental capacity to complete these chores and the value of doing it together.

Managing Aggressive Behavior. In managing aggressive behavior, as depicted in the opening example, competent workers create a positive atmosphere with self-confidence and awareness. They recognize their fears and anxieties, yet can say *no* with a sense of conviction and certainty. They control with their presence, rather than with fear or threats.

At the same time, they try to understand the meaning of the youth's behavior. They ask themselves: How is he or she feeling? What does the world or situation look like through his or her lens? Is his or her assessment of what's going on the same as mine? From his or her perspective, what purpose does this behavior serve? Is my response, nonresponse, action, or reaction, appropriate? Is my time, sense of movement, or rhythm compatible with resolving the situation? Am I moving too fast or too slow? Am I too loud or not definite enough? How does the room or space we are in contribute to the behavior? Should I move away from the table, raise the lights, get into an open or closed area?

Conducting Transitions. Workers pay special attention to timing, mood, tone, and movement as they go from one activity to the next. They simultaneously try to understand the meaning of what went before, what comes after, and what's going on in the present; foreshadow and ask how fast or slow to move; judge their proximity to others (who should I be close to, further away from); and sense the elasticity of the space (is it too tight or loose) between themselves and each youth and how it relates to safety.

Planning Activities. In selecting, planning, and implementing activities, workers consider each youth's developmental capacity and readiness to participate. They develop a wide repertoire of activities and choose activities that are challenging and exciting, but not overtaxing. During the activity, the workers are engaged in activities with youth. They adjust the tempo, sound, pace, and space, so they can learn as best as possible together.

An art project or a game of volleyball, for instance, is chosen because youth have the emotional, physical, and cognitive ability to participate in the project or game. Then, during the project of game, the worker is sensitive to tempo, time, place, and motivation.

Learning in Context

Workers get a feel for context and develop their technique through trial-and-error experiences with youth. They reflect on and analyze a situation to see how it might be enhanced or repeated. A supervisor or a colleague, for example, helps a worker understand the meaning of a confrontation, or a moment of excitement, and how the worker handled the situation.

A youth was angry because he failed a test earlier or lost at a game of basketball. Another youth was excited because he had just heard that his father would be taking him to the movies that evening, or because he was winning at a video game. The worker stepped in too soon or too late or at just the right time. He or she chose the right or the wrong technique for the situation. In hindsight, the worker might have been handled a situation the same or differently. Next time, the worker will repeat his or her actions or choose new ones. And so forth.

To provide a context for learning in the classroom, teachers often demonstrate, interact, and discuss. Maier [1987], a pioneer in teaching youth work in context, arrives early for a workshop to make sure the room or space in which learning will occur is properly arranged. To set the tone, he greets participants as they arrive, trying to get to know them the way youth workers might try to get to know new youth. He welcomes them, "I'm glad you're here."

During a workshop, he stands within a circle and shifts his position as he leads, guides, and/or observes. He sits or stands in the front of the group to describe a concept or technique, then pauses to invite discussion. He gives feedback. He moves from one group to another during a small group role play or problem-solving exercise, helping out.

Fewster [1990] engages workers in a dialogue and encourages them to learn from their experience with youth. He frames and reframes with colorful images, debates with humor and wit, challenges, and speaks with passion.

Similarly, effective mentors and supervisors role model, demonstrate, conduct dialogues, and frame and reframe a situation to find common meaning. Like Maier, they welcome others to the learning process. They teach a technique by modeling it, or by discussing a hypothetical case example. They accent learning during daily interactions by stepping back together, reflecting, and analyzing a situation to see how it might be enhanced or repeated.

An Example. I recently lead a 16-week class for 10 student youth workers, and framed the class as a conversation. On the first day, we sat together in a circle and began to get to know each other. I explained that we would try to interact with one another the way we wanted to learn to interact with youth and their family members. We would try to listen to one another and support and confront one another with care. We would also try to hold each other accountable and try to be dependable and predictable [Maier 1987].

During the class, we used several methods to enhance our conversation. For example, using the dance metaphor introduced in the previous essay, we discussed youth workers as moving through the day trying to stay in sync with youth's rhythms for trusting and growing. We thought of the ebb and flow of the work. How youth work, like modern dance, was both choreographed and improvised.

I suggested that youth work was mainly a process of self in action. Worker and youth being real. Worker and youth acting with purpose. Worker and youth becoming aware. Worker and youth in and out of sync with each other's rhythms for trusting and growing. Worker and youth in time and space. And workers teaching and empowering youth by being and acting in harmony with self while integrating care and learning into interactions. We discussed these ideas.

We role played [Maier 1989] and problem solved. We practiced techniques, such as praise and discipline. We also watched two movies about youth; wrote stories of moments of change, sadness, joy, etc.; toured an agency; and discussed what we had experienced.

One day we practiced transitioning. We broke into two groups. One student played the role of a worker; the rest of the group members pretended they were youth. The challenge was to move the group from the game room to dinner. The group members gave the worker a hard time. One youth couldn't find his shoe. Another didn't like what was on the menu. And another quit the game of checkers he was playing.

After we role played the situation, we talked about the importance of preparation, the meaning of the activities, timing in moving, and the tone and atmosphere of the room. Then we went back and practiced again with the awareness that smooth transitions were instrumental in helping youth cope with change and in creating a flow to the day.

Another day, we role played a group discussion about drugs. One participant played the role of the worker and six participants played the roles of youth. At one point in the discussion, one of the youth asked the worker, "What about you? I'll bet you used drugs?" The purpose for the question was to put the worker on the spot. The challenge was for the worker to respond with a sense of sincerity, awareness, and self-confidence, so that the conversation could be shifted back to the youth.

In a discussion about youth at risk, we tried to understand the meaning of their stories [Bruner 1990; Peterson 1994; Saleeby 1994]. We asked ourselves: What does it mean to live in a world of violence? What does it mean to trust someone when everyone else has broken your trust? What does it mean to put your head on the pillow at night and have thoughts of failure and abuse race through your mind? Do the headphones and music help drown out the thoughts? Does a dirty track suit serve as a security blanket for a sexually abused body? Is a gang symbol a symbol of belonging?

If a youth keeps returning to a detention center because he can get three square meals and a dry bed, what is it like where he lives? How does culture define a youth? If a youth's relatives do not believe in self-disclosure outside the family, what does it feel like to be asked to disclose in a peer group or therapy session? For a youth who has been rejected as a runner by a drug lord because he is old enough to be prosecuted, what kind of crazy world does this youth live in?

We told our own stories. In a writing exercise, we wrote about moments of happiness, sadness, enthusiasm, success, failure, and loss. Then we talked about how these moments influenced who we are and how we interpreted events.

We talked across the spaces of our experience [Sarris 1993]. We said, "This is what it seems like to me. What does it feel like for you? When I was in that situation, here's how I reacted. How would you react?"

Then we explored situations: A youth lives in a neighborhood where several of his friends have been shot. A youth comes from a "to be" versus a "to do" culture [Weaver 1990]. A youth has been abused by an adult he loves. Then we asked: What is this experience like in comparison to my experience? What can I learn from my experience that will help me understand?

We acknowledged that actions count as much, if not more than, words. For example, when a youth and a youth worker are playing together and laughing, the shared rhythm lends to the formation of their connection in the moment [Krueger 1995; Maier 1992]. We tried to determine how actions, surroundings, and words contributed to or inhibited growth. We asked, How do facial expressions, motions, and words support or contradict the interactions?

We discussed how sometimes nothing is more telling than a sigh or smile. We considered the meaning of everyday actions: He swept the floor. He got up from his chair. He joined the activity. She moved closer to the other girl. He started to back pedal.

In practicing techniques, we tried to get a sense of how actions fit with a story of a moment or event or activity. When is it time to step in or stand aside? When is it best to say something or not something? What's the story here? Is their/my behavior consistent with what happened/is happening? Are we (I) responding with forethought and intuition to support or advance or change the action?

We discussed how space influenced our interactions. We paid special attention to temperature, lights, sunlight, open and closed windows, etc. Although there were limitations, we made the best of our surroundings.

As the teacher, I tried to set a positive tone. I smiled and spoke enthusiastically.

The students seemed to respond. When someone appeared down or disinterested, I changed the approach or subject to capture his or her interest. Most of the time, we tried to engage everyone in our discussions, but sometimes we simply respected each other's space and left one another alone.

At the beginning of most classes, we spent a few moments covering current events. I asked the participants to read the paper and watch the news, then we talked about key issues in schools and neighborhoods and families, such as guns and violence, school dropouts, and teen pregnancy. We also discussed examples of exemplary practice—good schools, programs, and workers. We tried to envision ourselves as part of this larger world of youth work. We searched for solutions to problems and took notes on how to integrate the successes into our own repertoire of approaches and techniques.

We also broke into two work groups and designed two model programs, a community center and a shelter. I encouraged them to be idealistic and to build in what they had learned from the course. The outcomes were excellent. Afterwards, we agreed that these would be good places for youth.

Finally, with the awareness that youth work interactions are complex, we tried to look at the uniqueness and interrelatedness of micro- and macro-events—it was as if we were looking through a kaleidoscope. As we sifted and sorted through our experiences during and in between classes, certain patterns or insights often emerged. "Yes, now I can see what you mean," we said.

Summary

In youth work, all interactions take place in a unique context. Competence includes the ability to understand and act with sensitivity to any number of factors, circumstances, and meanings that contribute to the context in which an interaction takes place. This is a challenge that requires experience, knowledge, and practice to address.

References & Recommended Readings

Arieli, M. (1996). Do Alabama and New Moab belong to the same universe? *Child and Youth Care Forum, 25*, 289-292.

Baizerman, M. (1996). Can we get there from here: A comment on Shealy. *Child and Youth Care Forum, 25*, 285-288.

Baizerman, M. (1993). Response: Conversation by context. *Child and Youth Care Forum, 22*, 241-244.

Beker, J., Gittleson, P., Husted, S., Kaministein, P., & Finkler-Adler, L. (1972). *Critical incidents in child care: A case study book.* New York: Behavioral Publications.

Bruner, J. (1990). *Acts of Meaning.* Cambridge, MA.: Harvard University Press.

Childress, H. (1996). *Landscapes of betrayal, landscapes of joy: Curtisville in the lives of its teenagers.* Unpublished doctoral dissertation: University of Wisconsin-Milwaukee.

Fewster, G. (1990). *Being in child care: A journey into self.* New York: Haworth.

Freeman, A. (1993). Jacob and the preacher: Conversations in context. *Child and Youth Care Forum, 22*, 245-246.

Garfat, T. (1995). *The effective child and youth care intervention: A phenomenological inquiry.* Doctoral dissertation, University of Victoria, British Columbia.

Jacobs, H. (1996). The direct care practice concentration: A new development in the education of direct care practitioners. *The Journal of Child and Youth Care Work, 10,* 37-53.

Krueger, M. (1995). *Nexus: A book about youth work.* Milwaukee, WI: University Outreach Press, University of Wisconsin-Milwaukee, in cooperation with Child Welfare League of America.

Maier, H. (1995). Genuine child care practice across the North American continent. *Journal of Child and Youth Care, 10,* 11-22.

Maier, H. (1992). Rhythmicity: A powerful force for experiencing unity and personal connections. *Journal of Child and Youth Care Work, 8,* 7-14.

Maier, H. (1989). Role playing: Structures and educational objectives. *Journal of Child and Youth Care, 4,* 41-37.

Maier, H. (1987). *Developmental group care of children and youth.* New York: Haworth.

Peterson, R. (1994) The adrenaline metaphor: Narrative mind and practice in child and child and youth care. *Journal of Child and Youth Care,* 107-122.

Redl, F., & Wineman, D. (1957). *Controls from within: Techniques for treatment of the aggressive child.* New York: Free Press.

Richmond, P. (1998). Untitled paper for completion of an independent study in child and youth care. University of Wisconsin-Milwaukee.

Saleebey, D. (1994). Culture, theory, and narrative: The intersections of meaning in practice. *Social Work, 39,* 35-359.

Sarris, G. (1993). *Keeping Slug Woman alive: An holistic approach to American Indian texts.* Berkeley, CA: University of California Press.

Williams, P. (1995). *Developing a model to ease youth's transitions into residential treatment: Integrating constructivist therapies and youth care work into a contextually relevant rite of passage.* NOVA/Southeastern University: A master's practicum.

Weaver, G. (1990). The crisis of cross cultural child care. In M. Krueger & N. Powell (Eds.), *Choices in caring: Contemporary approaches to child and youth care* (pp. 65-101). Washington, DC: Child Welfare League of America.

Essay Three
Understanding

You are talking with someone, perhaps at a restaurant, or during a walk in a park. Suddenly you sense that he or she really understands what you are saying.

As you interact with youth during a game or routine or chore, you observe, sense, explore the meaning of interactions.

The major challenge in the interactive approach is to understand. Competent workers are infinitely curious. It is their quest to understand, perhaps more than any other facet of youth work, that seems to invite connections, relationships, and growth.

Recently a number of qualitative researchers and youth workers have described how they use self, story, and/or intuition to gain a deeper understanding of their experiences and interactions. In this essay, these methods will be described for further exploration.

Self as Part of the Journey

In the introduction to his collection of essays describing his ethnographies of spiritual healers, anthropologist Greg Sarris wrote about Mabel McKay, a Pomo Indian basket weaver and medicine woman:

> It is important that I remember my life, my presence and history as I attempt to understand Mabel. As I learn more

> about Mabel, I learn more about myself. In this way using much of what Mabel taught me, I show these essays myself and others learning, seeing beyond what seems to be. [Sarris 1993, p. 5]

Sarris, like other qualitative researchers, was acknowledging the importance of using his presence or self to understand [Fewster 1990; Garfat 1995; Moustakas 1990, 1994; Sarris 1993]. Rather than take the position that researchers have to remove themselves from a situation to be objective, these researchers believe that an awareness of their experiences and feelings leads to a deeper understanding of the meaning of what is occurring.

In describing heuristic research, a method he uses to understand such feelings and phenomenon as love, loneliness, rituals, rhythms, and relationships, Moustakas wrote:

> The self of the researcher is present throughout the process and, while understanding the phenomenon with increasing depth, the researcher also experiences growing self-awareness and self-knowledge.... In heuristics, an unshakable connection exists between what is out there, in its appearance and reality, and what is in me in reflective thought, feeling, and awareness. [Moustakas 1994, pp. 9-11]

Other forms of qualitative research, such as hermeneutics and field study, discuss the importance of including self in the process of study [Garfat 1995; Husserl 1970; Moustakas 1994; Peterson 1994]. These writers argue that reality, or the true meaning of an experience, can only be fully understood through an awareness of inner feelings and consciousness.

In the field of child and youth care work, Fewster [1990, 1991] and others [Baizerman 1995; Garfat 1995; Rose Sladde 1996] have written eloquently about youth work as a shared journey. The major task, they argue, is to understand the subjective world of the youth by sharing the road to self-discovery. In their novels, essays, and columns, they articulate how workers use their experience to understand and be with youth. To understand a youth's fear, sadness, loss, trauma, joy, for instance, workers have to be able to understand how they experience these emotion themselves, so they can understand how their feelings influence their understanding of and contribute to their interactions with youth.

In *Being in Child Care: A Journey into Self*, a story based on a worker's conversation with his supervisor, Fewster wrote:

> Charlotte was inviting me to consider the idea that self-examination and discovery is a process of observing self in action. At the broader level this is compatible with the preference for cerebral realms of theory and philosophy to follow experience ... The idea is that when we are experiencing another person, particularity at the feeling or emotional level, we are actually experiencing ourselves. [Fewster, 1990, pp. 42, 147]

In a column titled, "Journal Entries," Rose Sladde discussed how her feelings had biased her interactions with a challenging boy, and how through understanding these feelings she was better able to understand his actions. At the end of her column she wrote:

> I have learned, as I write this, that the medium of self-reflection and understanding is critical to my professional field. If we are to work with troubled children and youth, we have to become aware of who we are as individuals. [Rose Sladde 1996, p. 82]

Thus, many workers and researchers include themselves in the process. They ask: How does my experience influence what I see? How do my current feelings influence the way I interpret an interaction? How is my world different than the world of the youth and families? How is it the same? How does my presence influence the situation? What can I learn from my experience with others that will help me understand the true meaning of it?

In asking these questions, workers and researchers are not trying to exclude or weed out their experiences and biases, but rather, they are trying to understand how they contribute to an interaction or situation. They become part of an event or interaction and use themselves to gain a deeper understanding of the meaning of that event or interaction.

Stories as a Frame

Workers or researchers often frame their experiences and observations in a story. For instance, when observing or reflecting on an experience or writing a log or report [Garfat 1995; Moustakas 1994; Peterson 1994; Sarris 1993], they ask: What is the story of my experience or observation ? In what context did that interaction or event occur? How has my experience influenced the way I perceive the story? How does this story fit with a series of previous stories? How might a youth view the story differently based on his or her evolving story? How do the stories fit with the evolving story of youth work and the individuals within it?

This form of analysis is supported by psychologists, sociologists, anthropologists, and practitioners who argue that the way we build ourselves into the world or make meaning of our experiences is based on the story that evolves from familial, cultural, and communal experiences [Bruner 1990; Rapoport 1990; Saleebey 1994; Sarris 1993]. Bruner, for instance, discusses at length how we make sense of the world based on "the rough and changing draft of our autobiography that we carry in our minds" [1990, p. 33].

As researchers/workers try to understand the stories they observe and experience, they seem to have at least three thoughts in mind. First, the story of what is occurring is unique, because they are there, and this story would not be the same if they weren't there. Second, the story gains existence from its occurrence and their (themselves and others) recollection of it. And third, the way they (themselves and others) interpret the story is based on their cultural and familial experience [Bruner 1990].

For example, a researcher or worker is sitting down to eat with a group of youth. The story of the meal will include the researcher or worker, because he or she is there and it would not be the same story without that worker. After some reflection, the story of the meal will later take on a different meaning. It will not be exactly the same as it was. All of the participants will recall the story of the meal in a different way, based on what they remember and how they have experienced meals before.

The meal in this context has multiple meanings. For youth who are not used to sitting down to dinner with others, or who are not used to having food served to them, or who are used to eating at different times in different atmospheres, the meal will have a different meaning than for youth for whom the experiences are more familiar.

To understand the meanings of these shared and separate experiences, workers and researchers speak with others across the spaces of their experience [Sarris 1993; Moustakas 1994; Garfat 1995]. Garfat [1995], for instance, argued that workers and youth have their own ways of making sense of an interaction and the context in which it occurs, and that workers must try to understand the youth's contextual reality through dialogue. Sarris [1993] argued that cultural biases influence the translation of events and that something is usually lost (much the way we lose meaning in the translation of language), unless the researcher enters a dialogue with his or her subjects.

In the dialogue, worker and researcher ask: How do you see it? What is it like from your perspective? Is this an example of what you mean? The worker/researcher also recasts or reframes the story, suggesting it is like this or perhaps that, searching for common ground or reality.

Words alone, however, do not tell a story. In his classic study of how individuals present themselves to others, Goffman wrote,

> The expressiveness of the individual (and therefore his capacity to give impressions) appears to involve two radically different kinds of sign activity: the expression that he gives and the impression that he gives off. [Goffman 1959, p. 2]

In searching for the meaning of a story, workers and researchers also try to understand the meaning of participants' actions. For example, as suggested in the example at the beginning of "Essay Two: Context," when a youth "is in another youth's face," what appears to be the start of a fight might instead be part of a street ritual that is a competition of wit, rather than fists. When a youth and a youth worker are jogging together and laughing, the shared rhythm lends to the formation of their connection in the moment [Krueger 1994 & 1995; Maier 1992]. A smile might be an expression of joy or a cover for fear or uncertainty.

In literature, description and dialogue are used to advance the story. Similarly, workers and researchers analyze interactions to determine how actions, surroundings, and words contribute to or inhibit growth or relationships [Krueger 1995; Moustakas 1990, 1994]. In other words, how do facial expressions, motions, and words support or contradict the interactions? Sometimes nothing is more telling than a sigh or smile or action—such as getting up from a chair and joining the activity.

Intuition

Researchers and workers also rely on intuition. They experience and look with intensity at the interrelatedness of micro- and macro-events and the truth or reality that is created with the addition of feeling and intuitive thought [Bruner 1990]. They simultaneously interact, experience, observe, and look back; interact, experience, observe, and look back.

In what he defines as entering into self-dialogue, Moustakas [1990], argues that to know a phenomenon we must engage in a rhythmic flow with it, and move back and forth again and again until we discover multiple meanings. To understand the wholeness and unique patterns of experience [Fewster 1990; Moustakas 1990], workers and researchers often move from specific to general and back again. Quoting Craig, Moustakas [1990] wrote, "From the feeling to the word and back to the feeling; from the experience to the concept and back to the experience" [Craig 1978, p. 57].

As we interact and reflect, sometimes it is as if we are looking through a kaleidoscope. As workers sift and sort through the data (observations, feelings, experiences), certain patterns or insights often emerge. Sometimes workers sense how a child feels based on previous experience. Or they interact with the material (thoughts, observations, notes, experiences) and mold it. They become part of the process, changing and becoming sensitive to how these changes influence the meaning of their interactions. Like sculpting with clay, they work the material with their hands and intuition, changing the shape until it looks and feels right. They sense, as well as see, what is going on.

Summary

Self, story, and intuition are used in many ways to understand daily interactions. Workers, for instance, learn as much as they can about adolescent development, get fully engaged in daily activities, and develop their senses and intellect for understanding. They interact, step back, reflect, record, communicate, and search—and then interact, step back, reflect, record, communicate, and search again. Sometimes they feel as much as know what is occurring, then later step back and search for patterns and/or even deeper meanings.

Workers also discuss and explore motives and meanings for actions together. Collective insight helps them delve into the multiple issues that create context and to avoid generalizations and stereotypes. They reinforce the value of understanding as the core of connecting and successful intervention, challenge one another to see a situation from a different perspective, and explore the themes or meanings of a story through a different lens. Workers and youth become, through communication, open and willing to accept different points of view, panels of experts, guided by intuition, skill, knowledge, and the capacity to see.

Thus, in the context presented here, understanding, like youth work, is also largely a process of self in action [Fewster 1990]. Researcher/worker trying to experience being with children and youth. Researcher/worker searching through dialogue, action, and reflection for the meaning of an event or story. And researcher/worker trying to capture the flow, feel, and sense of what is occurring. Understanding this process further, it seems to me, is one of the more intriguing challenges in knowing youth work.

References & Recommended Readings

Baizerman, M. (1995). The secret of life. *Child and Youth Care Forum, 24,* 209-210.

Bruner, J. (1990). *Acts of meaning.* Cambridge, MA: Harvard University Press.

Craig, E. (1978). The heart of the teacher: A heuristic study of the inner world of teaching. *Dissertation Abstracts International, 38,* 7222A.

Fewster, G. (1990). *Being in child care: A journey into self.* New York: Haworth.

Fewster, G. (1991). The paradoxical journey: Some thoughts on relating to children. *Journal of Child and Youth Care,* v-ix

Garfat, T. (1995). *The effective child and youth care intervention: A phenomenological inquiry.* Doctoral dissertation, University of Victoria, British Columbia.

Goffman, I. (1959). *The presentation of self in everyday life.* New York: Doubleday.

Husserl, E. (1970). *Logical investigations.* New York: Humanities Press.

Krueger, M. (1994). Framing child and youth care in moments of rhythm, presence, meaning, and atmosphere. *Child and Youth Care Forum, 23,* 223-229.

Krueger, M. (1995). *Nexus: A book about youth work.* Milwaukee, WI: Outreach Press, University of Wisconsin-Milwaukee, in partnership with Child Welfare League of America.

Maier, H. (1992). Rhythmicity: A powerful force for experiencing unity and personal connections. *Journal of Child and Youth Care Work, 8,* 7-14.

Moustakas, C. (1990). *Heuristic research: Design, methodology, and applications.* Newberry Park, CA: Sage Publications.

Moustakas, C. (1994). *Phenomenological research methods.* Chicago: University of Chicago Press.

Peterson, R. (1994). The adrenaline metaphor: Narrative mind and practice in child and child and youth care. *Journal of Child and Youth Care, 9,* 107-122.

Polyani, M. (1969). *Knowing and being.* (Marjorie Greene, Ed.) Chicago: University of Chicago Press.

Rapoport, A. (1990). *The meaning of the built environment.* Tucson, AZ: University of Arizona Press.

Rose Sladde, L. (1996). Journal entries. *Journal of Child and Youth Care, 10,* 79-83.

Saleebey, D. (1994). Culture, theory, and narrative: The intersection of meanings in practice. *Social Work, 39,* 35-359.

Sarris, G. (1993). *Keeping Slug Woman alive: An holistic approach to American Indian texts.* Berkeley, CA: University of California Press.

Vander Ven, K., Mattingly, M., & Morris, M. (1982). Principles and guidelines for child care preparation programs. *Child Care Quarterly, 11,* 221-244.

Walcott, H. (1992) On seeking-and rejecting-validity in qualitative research. In E. Eisner & A. Peshkin (Eds.), *Qualitative inquiry in education: The continuing debate* (pp. 121-152). New York: Teachers College Press.

Weaver, G. (1990). The crisis of cross cultural child and youth care. In M. Krueger & N. Powell, (Eds.), *Choices in caring* (pp. 65-101). Washington, DC: Child Welfare League of America.

Essay Four

Four Themes

Four themes—presence, meaning, rhythm, and atmosphere—permeate workers' interactions with youth [Krueger 1995, 1994].

Presence

On Friday, Joy and I talked
about sense of presence.
What is it? How does it come about?
I think it has to do
with a sense of worth, dignity,
and how you fit with occasion, place,
people, and time.
It is also a physical thing,
carriage of body,
head and hand movements,
eyes fixed upon specific points.
And then it is an ability
which is instinctive and spiritual
to convey what you see

to those around you.

Essentially, it is how you fit

into the space which is yourself,

how well and how appropriately.

This section of a poem by Simon Ortiz [1992, p. 126], the Native Ameri-can poet, beautifully defines presence. Presence is a sense of dignity and worth and the ability to fit into the space that is yourself. In work with youth, having a sense of presence is often referred to as being "real." Work-ers with presence are internally and externally consistent. Their actions, words, and feelings are in harmony. They bring themselves to the moment.

Presence is conveyed in many ways. By eyes, smiles, and nods that are alert and attentive. By listening. By an honest expression of a feeling. By enthusiasm for the task at hand. By the underlying message: We can move forward together, you and I. I am confident we can make it. You are safe because I am here and will go with you. I will try to know myself if you will try to know yourself.

Following are examples of presence in youth work.

At the community center a middle-aged man stands at a workbench with three youth around him. He sands a piece of wood as the youth sand their wood. He stops and stands behind each one, making a comment or helping. They work separately at times and together at other times. They seem to fill the space in which they are working.

A worker is listening. His eyes are focused on a youth.

Several workers are discussing a program plan with a group of youth. They are sitting in a circle facing one another. Each worker is engaged in the conversation, listening and speaking with a sense of conviction and seriousness about the task at hand.

A worker stands firmly between two youth who are arguing.

A worker and a youth walk through the neighborhood. Another worker stands next to a group of youth folding clothes. They are together in the moment.

I have observed many people who seem to convey a sense of presence. Here are a few descriptions of some of them.

Tina was a short, but proud woman who conveyed a strong sense of confidence. When she said no, she meant no. She didn't threaten or bribe. She simply meant no and it came across with the conviction that she could and would do whatever she had to do to make the youth safe and keep them involved in activities.

Nick was a war vet; youth work was a second career. The words he chose might not have been the ones a "professional" would have chosen, but the words, combined with his actions, seemed to be understood by youth as meaning that he cared about them. The kids wanted to be with him. On camping trips, they huddled around him at the fire and eagerly joined him in the canoe.

Josh, a new worker, was soft spoken and thoughtful. He came across as wanting to understand. Sometimes the kids gave him a hard time, but they seemed to trust him.

Majorie was a proud Native American woman. She stood straight and emanated a sense of inner peace, as well as concern. Her struggle as a minority woman had made her stronger, rather than hard and angry. In the craft room she moved and spoke with dignity and enthusiasm for her work. The youth seemed to pick up on this as they put themselves into their paintings and craft projects.

Ramone devoted himself to his work. It was his cause. He began in Vista and then moved into a community-based program. Although the work did not come as easily to him as to some of his colleagues, he was always trying to improve and learn. The youth seemed to relate to this desire to do his work as best as he could.

Mack's words came out in a poetry of phrases he'd stored up over the years. His expertise was storytelling and recreation. The kids always seemed engaged with him in a game or a conversation. Although perhaps not "hip" in current youth culture, his "coolness" seemed to come from who he was, not an act of some kind.

In summary, presence is a sense of dignity and worth, a oneness with the space that is yourself, a quest to know and accept yourself and others, and a desire and capacity to be present for and with youth.

The most important lesson I've learned during the past six months is the importance of staying present in the moment [Fewster 1990, p. 140].

Meaning

Meaning is the sense that youth and workers make of the world around them. The reality that guides their choices. The cultural and familial experiences that help them shape and build themselves into the world. Meaning is also the purpose they attach to their actions. The meaning with which they act.

There are usually many potential meanings for a youth's behavior and/or how he or she interprets others actions [Bruner 1990; Weaver 1990]. Using methods of understanding, such as those described in the previous essay, workers try to place themselves in youth' shoes and see the world through their eyes. They ask questions:

- How does the world look through his or her unique lens? How does a youth feel, understand, and behave, based on his or her developmental (social, emotional, cognitive, and physical) skills, strengths, and weaknesses?

- What influence are his or her peers having in creating a sense of joy, anticipation, or struggle?

- Is what we are doing together meaningful—and what is the meaning based on how the youth has previously experienced in similar situations? How is this meal, game of checkers, hike, jog, art project, way of getting up in the morning, or song perceived, based on the rituals and traditions of the youth's family and culture?

- How do fear, anxiety, excitement, exuberance influence behavior?

- What is he or she saying in his or her, art, dance, music?

Workers also try to understand the story behind youth's actions:

Baseball is meaningful to a girl because her mother was a good athlete and she wants to be like her mother. Her aggressive playing is partially a way of demonstrating how important it is to her to do well.

A girl reorganizes and decorates her room. Each object, the dresser, the bed, the jewelry box, the photos on the wall are an expression of who she is. The colors and tones and the slightly abstracted view of the room describe how she often feels in her space.

A boy hangs out at the mall with his friends, because it is a space where something might happen. Often nothing happens, but it is the possibility that someone might come or something might occur that is new and exciting.

A girl dabbles with her food, eats slowly, talks endlessly. In her family, meals are a social event that often runs into evening conversations.

A youth in a transitional living group home throws a rock through the bay window the day he is supposed to leave to return to live in the community. What seems like self-defeating behavior to others is the only way the youth knows how to say he is not ready to go. He is more frightened of being back on the streets than he is of the consequences he will face at the transitional living group home.

A teenager gets pregnant without thinking about the consequences. Having a child, she believes, is the only way she can make a contribution of some kind and have someone who will care for her. Besides she will receive money and attention for this contribution, as have many of her peers. She has no sense of how much work it will be. Nor how inadequate the money will be.

With an awareness of and/or sense of curiosity about the meaning or possible meanings of an event or interaction, workers try to act with purpose [Bruner 1990]. They butter a piece of bread, button or unbutton a collar, speak a phrase, bounce a ball, or hold a fork in a certain way, because it has purpose. Or they solve a problem or make an effort in a way they believe will lead to the best results. Sometimes the meaning is different for worker and youth, but their relationship is strengthened or a skill learned because they are doing something meaningful together.

A worker listens to a youth's story about his father as they work side by side on two drawings. The worker is trying to understand the youth's story. He listens and simultaneously draws. Both are engaged in what they are doing.

Rhythm

Rhythm is beat, motion, tempo. It is part of most interactions. A hand moving to pass a bowl or food or away from a shoulder to draw a youth along. A transition from one activity to the next. A game of catch.

In an article on rhythmicity, Maier wrote the following:

> Have you noticed that when people jog, dance or throw a Frisbee in rhythm with each other, they seem to experience momentary bonding and a sense of unity. At these and other moments of joint rhythmic engagement, they discover an attraction for each other regardless of whether there has been a previous sense of caring. In fact, it is almost impossible to dislike a person while being rhythmically in "sync." Rhythmic interactions forge people together. Rhythmicity provides a glue for establishing human connections.... [Maier 1992, p. 7]

Hall [1976] defined the role of rhythm in communication, noting that when people talk to one another, their movements are synchronized in sometimes barely perceptible ways (such as eye blinking) and in other cases, bodies move as if under the "control of a master choreographer."

> Viewing movies (of the details of communication) in very slow motion, looking for synchrony, one realizes that what we know as dance is really a slowed-down stylized version of what humans do whenever they interact. [Hall 1976, p. 49]

Csikzsentmahalyi [1990] discusses the joys of movement and rhythm in reaching optimal experience, likening it to experiences of dancers and athletes. The sense of floating along, having fun, just moving around.

For instance, I remember running. Running early in the morning at camp with a group of early risers—the specialness of sharing the privacy of sunrise and the surrounding country as we moved together silently, listening to the birds, the sound of our feet hitting the ground, and our own breath. Or, flowing over the sidewalks with a youth who had been quite difficult to connect with and for the first time feeling a sense of togetherness.

Interactive workers try to be in sync. They strive for interactions that have a rhythmic quality. They are intuitively and consciously aware of the importance of rhythm and movement. Like modern dancers, they have a sense for the changing beat, as well as the planned and improvised mood the dance is trying to create. They are aware of when their voices should be firm or gentle, when it's time to be in the center of the group or at the edge, when the pace of movement from one activity to the next is too fast or too slow, when energy is fresh or almost spent.

They also plan their interactions and activities with sensitivity to rhythm. They introduce a game of catch at a time when children are bored or restless. In their activity planners, music, dance, gymnastics, walks, runs, and role plays have a central place.

In a broader sense, an argument can be made that interacting with youth is a matter of getting in sync with their rhythms for trusting and growing. Each youth has a unique readiness and capacity to grow [Maier 1987]. These rhythms cannot be forced. Workers strive to find the proper pace—a pace that is in tune with youth's temperaments and geared to the emotional, physical, social, and cognitive strengths of the child or youth—then move through the activity guiding, encouraging, challenging, counseling, and/or learning with them.

In discussing a day at Forest Heights Lodge in Colorado, Fahlberg wrote:

> As everyone, adults and boys alike, takes a seat in the living room, a new calmer rhythm is set. The more hurried pace of early morning activity is replaced by a slower more relaxed tempo. Voice levels are softened, movements are not so hurried. It is the adults' responsibility to facilitate this change in the rhythms of the group.... [Fahlberg 1990, p. 172]

Things, of course, don't always go smoothly. Frequently, workers and youth struggle to get in sync, as is depicted in these excerpts from a story about a shift with an inexperienced worker:

> We develop a quick plan and get ready. He's got good energy, good intentions, but doesn't know the group. This makes things harder for both of us, but we seem to work well together. It feels good. Things start to come together...

> We go crazy all night. Two fights, a few arguments, one runaway returned by police, a visit from a neighbor who thinks the kids stole his lawn mower, too many irrelevant phone calls, not enough food thawed for dinner, an angry mother, a depressed newcomer and no breaks for us. Ronald and I struggle through....

> It's nine o'clock before we get everyone in the common room for a group discussion. A bit of yelling, some tears, and finally some understanding. Things cool down. The program's back on track by ten....

> Gradually the house starts to fall silent. The radios play softly. There's the odd giggle and whisper. One by one the lights go out. It looks as if we made it.... [Desjardins & Freeman 1991, pp. 139-144]

In a story about the complexities of making a decision to intervene in an escalating event, Garfat wrote:

> So, Mark and Larry have got a little rhythm going here and Maria is feeding it. Yup, Mark just glanced over at her and Larry did a second ago, she's locked into all this, all right. [Garfat 1995, p. 56]

Maier [1992] suggested that sometimes we have to learn to listen, to look, and to explore in new ways to find the "pulse" of a group of youth. The noise in the dining room might be part of a song that holds together, rather than divides, the group. The excitement in the game room might be a commitment for some kind of joint activity. The art of working with children is in part being able to decide almost intuitively when these sounds and movements have reached the peak for engagement; the point beyond which the dance becomes counterproductive.

> Pure encounter! Jazz improvisation, not formal ballet, should
> be the metaphor: practice and practice so as to be ready to
> play as one is called upon by oneself, others, and the mo-
> ment to do, rather than so as to be able to do "just right" that
> which was practiced [Baizerman 1993, p. 245].

The following observation at a picnic for youth and youth workers from several community and neighborhood organizations depicts rhythm in youth work practice.

In attendance were about 25 youth workers, who had just completed a continuing education class, and 75 youth. They were scattered throughout the picnic area and nearby basketball courts. Some sat at picnic tables talking while the lunch was being prepared. Others played table games. Four or five went over to the courts.

One worker began a game of volleyball with a group of five boys and girls from community centers. Three youth on one side and two youth and the youth worker on the other side. They hit the ball back and forth, loosening up and talking. There were no rules. No one kept score. They hit the ball on the fly or on the bounce without paying too much attention to winning or losing.

The youth worker's voice, enthusiasm, position, and motion seemed to hold the others loosely around him in a configuration that expanded and contracted. He laughed with the children at their mistakes and complimented each one in a different way for effort and/or results. "Nice hit," or "Good try," he said, altering his tone, and accenting his comments with phrases such as "Whooo!" or "Hey!"

Other youth began to join in. The youth worker created front and back rows, having players shift periodically from front row to back. The "in" spot seemed to be near the net.

The worker picked up the loose ball and threw it to someone who had not hit it for a while, then encouraged the player to knock it over the net.

Or he pointed or called out a name so the other children fed the ball to someone on the fringe of the activity....

Atmosphere

Atmosphere is space, time, surroundings. It is also tone and mood. Like the themes of presence, meaning, and rhythm, atmosphere permeates and plays many roles in interactions. A light turned down to quiet the group. A radio turned up to invigorate. Rooms decorated with youth's paintings and posters to encourage expression and to help provide a sense of safety and familiarity. Reds, blues, and yellows to liven things up. Earth tones to ground. Chairs placed in a circle to facilitate discussion and participation. A room or hallway sized properly for an activity. A window left open or closed for comfort.

Workers create atmosphere with the tones of their voices. The expressions on their faces. A mood that sends off good vibes. A smile or laugh. A cry of excitement. An expression of jubilance or persistence. A sense of tenacity or "stick-to-it-tiveness." A sense of being and confidence that exudes permanence and safety. We are in this space, you and I, and together we create, change and shape it for our mutual benefit.

> We shape our buildings and they shape us.... Territory defines the person.... Whatever space supports the work endeavored, the question remains: in which way can spatial factors be altered to further accentuate the process.... [Maier 1987, pp. 59-62]

The space in which youth workers interact with youth contributes significantly to the success or failure of their interactions. It also says a lot about what is important in a program. At an international conference, I asked a group of workers who had returned from tours of U.S. agencies, what stood out for them as being different. A worker from France said that in the United States, we seem to focus a lot of our activities and spaces on the need to control youth rather than the need to create room or opportunity for expression. In his experience (as in the experience of workers from Denmark and Germany who were also engaged in the discussion), workers in their countries focused more attention on creative expression, with the belief that if they provide many opportunities for youth to express themselves, they will be less likely to need to do it aggressively.

I observed this tendency when I toured several U.S. agencies: the walls in a treatment center covered with carpeting to provide texture, but barren of pictures and drawings of youth, because, "We're going to keep this place nice"; the greeting area of a neighborhood center covered with paintings donated by donors who give a considerable amount of money to the agency.

I also observed spaces unfit for living: youth sleeping on the dirty floor of a detention center, mattresses in barren rooms, holes in walls, filth, metal detectors in dusty doorways.

In other locations, however, I noticed a great deal of sensitivity in making sure the environment included expressions of youth. In one treatment center, the youth collected weathered barn wood and paneled the walls, then hung their paintings and posters. In one city, a worker engaged youth in drawing murals under bridges and on buildings, instead of graffiti. In another, a Hispanic community center was alive with pictures and colors. It stood out in the neighborhood as a lively and safe place.

In discussing place, why kids hang in places like shopping malls, gang turf, and skinhead territory, Baizerman [1995a] wrote: "Place gives us meaning in the way it presents itself to us." Youth, he argues, hang in places where there is anticipation, the possibility that something can happen. The challenge in youth programs is to create spaces where there is a similar sense of anticipation, to find a balance between structure and discovery, to nurture curiosity and create a sense of intrigue, so youth are not bored or left with a sense that everything is predetermined.

In his work, *Landscapes of Betrayal, Landscapes of Joy: Curtisville in the Lives of Its Teenagers*, Childress [1996] suggested that youth also hang in places where they can discover their own uniqueness and dignity. Place in this context is where they feel and sense that they can *find self and be*. Workers who are *with* youth in these places can create opportunities for something good to happen. Together they can search for a greater sense of self.

As discussed in the second essay, youth workers create and adjust to context. With youth, they set the tone, stage, and mood by what they do, how they feel, and how they express how they feel. A worker's smile can brighten a moment; a moody worker can dampen a day. A worker chooses certain words and excludes others. The place in which these words are said (and how they are said) matters as much as the words themselves.

Turning again to the modern dance metaphor: the worker choreographs, then responds intuitively to the changing tempo of the music. What is the tone or mood we are trying to establish? How can the arrangement of space facilitate our play, discussion, or quiet time? What colors will be most stimulating, calming? What mood am I conveying and how does it influence the youth? How does a youth's mood influence my behavior? Is this a place where youth can find themselves and be?

The walls in the community center are covered with children's art work. From top to bottom it feels as if it is their place, a place where they can express who they are and where they're from and feel good about it. The atmosphere is alive with the excitement and enthusiasm of workers and youth. Many activities are planned in advance, but there is also a sense of possibility that something unpredictable might happen or someone new might show up. Kids come to hang and engage in a wide range of activities.

Nick, the youth worker, wants to talk quietly with Antonio, one of the youth, who seems upset about something. With a look of concern, he approaches Antonio and asks him if he would like to go into the lounge area to talk. Nick's voice is firm, yet reassuring. The lights in the lounge are down a bit and there is less commotion. It is also familiar. Antonio has been there several times to read magazines.

The group seems a little down. Mary raises the blinds and lets the sun fall across the floor, then turns down the radio and with voice slightly raised suggests that they go outside for a hike, moving slowly towards the door as she speaks and encourages.

References & Recommended Readings

Baizerman, M. (1993). Response: Conversation by context. *Child and Youth Care Forum, 22*, 3.

Baizerman, M. (1995a). Kids, place, and action (less). *Child and Youth Care Forum, 24*, 339-341.

Baizerman, M. (1995b). The secret of life. *Child and Youth Care Forum, 24*, 209-210.

Bruner, J. (1990). *Acts of meaning.* Cambridge, MA: Harvard University Press.

Childress, H. (1996). *Landscapes of betrayal, landscapes of joy: Curtisville in the lives of its teenagers.* Doctoral dissertation for the School of Architecture and Urban Planning, University of Wisconsin-Milwaukee.

Csikszentmihalyi, M. (1990). *Flow: The psychology of optimal experience.* New York: Harper and Row.

Desjardins, S., & Freeman, A. (1991). Out of synch. *Journal of Child and Youth Care, 6*, 139-144.

Fahlberg, V. (1990). *Residential treatment: A tapestry of many therapies.* Indianapolis, IN: Perspectives Press.

Fewster, G. (1990). *Being in child care: A journey into self.* New York: Haworth.

Garfat, T. (1995). *The effective child and youth care intervention: A phenomenological inquiry.* Doctoral dissertation, University of Victoria, British Columbia, Canada.

Hall, E. (1976). *Beyond culture.* Garden City, NY: Anchor Books.

Krueger, M. (1994). Framing child and youth care in moments of rhythm, presence, meaning, and atmosphere. *Child and Youth Care Forum, 23*, 223-229.

Krueger, M. (1995). *Nexus: A book about youth work.* Milwaukee, WI: Outreach Press, University of Wisconsin-Milwaukee, in partnership with Child Welfare League of America.

Maier, H. (1987). *Developmental group care of children and youth.* New York: Haworth.

Maier, H. (1992). Rhythmicity: A powerful force for experiencing unity and personal connections. *Journal of Child and Youth Care Work, 8,* 7-13.

Ortiz, S. (1992). *Woven stone.* Phoenix, AZ: University of Arizona Press.

Weaver, G. (1990). The crisis of cross cultural child care. In M. Krueger & N. Powell (Eds.), *Choices in caring: Contemporary approaches to child and youth care work* (pp. 65-101). Washington, DC: Child Welfare League of America.

Essay Five
A Guide for Daily Interactions

Using the information in the first three essays and the four themes in the previous essay as a guide, youth work practice can be thought of once again as a process of self in action. As workers interact with youth, they ask such questions as: Am I present? What is the meaning or purpose for the youth? For me? Are we in sync? How does or can atmosphere enhance or detract from our interactions? They then act accordingly.

Presence, for instance, is crucial to the success of most interactions. Workers try to be present with self-awareness, conviction, and enthusiasm. And so, we learn to ask: Am I present in the moment? How is my mood, enthusiasm, anger influencing the interaction? Am I focused on what's going on? Can the youth sense my conviction?

Workers also search for the meaning of youth's behavior. How is he or she feeling? What does the world or situation appear like through his or her lens? Is his or her assessment of what's going on the same or different than mine? From his or her perspective, what purpose does this behavior serve? Is my response, nonresponse, action or reaction, appropriate? Am I acting with purpose?

Is my timing, sense of movement, or rhythm compatible with the situation? Am I moving too fast or too slow? Am I too loud or not definite enough?

How is the room we are in or the outdoors contributing to the behavior? How can it enhance or detract from our involvement? Should I move away from the table, raise the lights, get into an open or closed area?

In effective listening, the worker is present. He or she shows an interest and tries to understand what is being said. The motion of the head and eyes is important, as is the atmosphere and context in which the listening is occurring.

In foreshadowing [Redl & Wineman 1957], a technique in which a worker enhances transitions by talking to youth about what they can expect in the future or next activity, the worker is sensitive to how she or he explains these events and what it means to each youth from his or her perspective. Is it something familiar, unfamiliar, frightening, exciting, etc? The worker also sets the tone with his or her own excitement or sense of assurance about the youth' ability to succeed together or individually. Workers assure youth that they or others will be with them.

In choosing an activity, a worker chooses one that is compatible with a youth's developmental ability and readiness, then gets fully engaged in the activity. Kickball is played instead of baseball because it is better suited to group members' physical skills, their ability to deal with delayed gratification, and their capacity to function in a team game that has winners and losers. An art project is chosen instead of a rap session, because the time, mood, and mode of expression are better suited to the current condition of the group members. Routines are scheduled with enough time and at a time that fits with the schedule for the rest of the day. Music, dance, and recreation activities are chosen with sensitivity to cultural and familial backgrounds.

In therapeutic encounters, youth anchor themselves in the presence of the others. They open up, because they feel safe with and connected to workers as they search together for meaning, often with the use of story and metaphor. Workers help construct a mutual reality as they try to re-solve a crisis or teach a skill. How do or did you see the situation? Tell me the story of what happened. Let's see if we can't find common ground for our discussion.

Peterson [1988], Redl [1959], and many others built the case for counsel-ing "on the go" [Krueger 1991], or seizing naturally occurring therapeutic opportunities. In this form of synchronicity, workers counsel at bedtime, after fights, or during dinner time when the feelings and behaviors are most immediate. They move together with youth, walk, sit quietly, listening and talking. The tone of the conversation and the space create a sense of safety and confidentiality. The timing for talk or to just be together is right.

Effective mentors and role models are internally consistent. We cannot pretend to be someone else or behave in a way that is inconsistent with who we are and/or what we are trying to teach or demonstrate. The men-tor has to be present with empathy and moving in synch with her or his internal rhythms and space.

In quiet moments together, the adult who is present is in the moment. In holding an aggressive youth or talking down two youth who are about to go to blows, successful interactions in part come from being able to feel the level of tension and when it is about to subside [Krueger 1987].

Rituals, such as meals, or evening songs, or household jobs, can be uni-fying experiences or arduous routines [Maier 1992]. The challenge is to find a balance of variety and predictability that is geared to the group members' developmental needs.

Presence and being present for rituals has a different meaning in differ-ent cultures. For some Native American youth, their being or presence might be more interrelated with their sense of family or community, while youth from another culture may be more concerned about what a person does for a living in society. For some youth, presence is more interrelated with time, space, and nature than for others. Presence on the street might have a different meaning than presence in an office. And so forth.

Workers try to be sensitive to the rhythm and meaning of a ritual as it relates to youth's cultural and familial experiences. The timing, pace, structure and atmosphere of a meal might be different for youth from an Italian, Puerto Rican, German, African American, or Pueblo community. Workers vary the rhythm of a prayer or song to begin or end a ceremony, to fit the rhythm of praying and singing in a variety of cultures. The timing of intervention in the ribbing and jiving of street kids might be different than the timing of intervention in the ritual of a teenager who comes from a culture where you hit first and argue later.

Holidays, greetings, good-byes (or lack of the notion of good-bye, as in some Native American cultures) have different meanings. The type of food and the way it is served. The colors of clothes at different ceremonies. Being present. Time. These and many other actions and symbols are important considerations in following rituals that help bond youth to workers and programs.

Transitions are designed to be a series of successful changes, comings and goings, beginnings and endings, enterings and leavings, in which youth can learn to count on and trust adults. Workers and youth move in harmony together from one activity to the next. The tempo of an activity or a facial expression changes. Workers in synch move with youth from the play yard to the dinner table, from showers to bed, from checkers to baseball, from the classroom to the recreation area, from the community center or group home to home.

In teaching social, job, and daily living routines, the adults who are present are engaged in the moment and activity. They are enthusiastic about and/or committed to the task at hand. The process of doing it together is more important than the outcome. They know what meaning the activity evokes in each youth.

Workers develop a feel for the elasticity of boundaries. Their presence conveys a sense of their space and comfort for others in the space, a willingness to get close or to keep some distance.

Workers also strive to understand the meaning of closeness, intimacy, and limits for youth. Each youth has developed a level of comfort in being with others based on his or her previous experiences and cultural traditions. Touch and structure are provided with sensitivity to these meanings. There is a natural flow to a hug. Spaces and rules whose elasticity reflects a youth's developmental readiness for expansion or contraction of boundaries.

A worker arrives early at the center to meet four youth who are waiting in their running clothes and shoes. They have been running together three times a week for several weeks. At first the youth didn't want to run; it was too tiring and too much work. Now they seem to wait eagerly for the worker.

Without saying anything they begin stretching together, then head out into the neighborhood. It takes a while to work out some of the stiffness. The neighborhood is familiar, and in places unsafe, but being together gives them confidence. The worker sets the pace. Together, they hold one another in a group, a loose configuration that gives each one enough space, yet keeps them in close enough proximity so they can gauge their speed according to one another's strides.

Once they are all breathing easily, they chat about school. Soon they are moving almost effortlessly. They run until the worker senses that a couple are getting tired. He slows the pace, then says, "Let's take a little breather." In the outfield of a baseball diamond at the local park, they walk, then sit down on the grass.

One youth says, "I don't think I'm going to the dance tonight."

"You're just scared, man," another youth says.

"No, I'm not!"

"Shit if you ain't. That woman you been looking at is gonna be there and you're worried she won't dig your ass."

"Shiiit, I don't even care."

"Why don't you come; I'll be there," the worker says.

References & Recommended Readings

Krueger, M. (1987). *Floating*. Washington, DC: Child Welfare League of America.

Krueger, M. (1991). Coming from your center, being there, teaming up, interacting together, meeting them where they're at, counseling on the go, creating circles of care, discovering and using self, and caring for one another: Central themes in child and youth care. *Journal of Child and Youth Care, 5*, 77-87.

Maier, H. (1992). Rhythmicity: A powerful force for experiencing unity and personal connections. *Journal of Child and Youth Care Work, 8*, 7-13.

Peterson, R. (1988). The collaborative metaphor technique: Using Ericsonian techniques and principles in child, family, and youth care work. *Journal of Child and Youth Care, 3*, 11-27.

Redl, F. (1959). Strategy and technique of the Life-Space Interview. *American Journal of Orthopsychiatry, 29*, 1-18.

Redl, F., & Wineman, D. (1957). *Controls from within: Techniques for treatment of the aggressive child*. New York: Free Press.

Practice Examples

The following examples were designed for discussion and practice in classrooms, supervision sessions, office discussions, training curriculum, and a variety of other learning situations.

Practice #1. Changing Tempo

The pushing and shoving in the basketball game is beginning to get out of hand. The worker grabs the ball and rests it on his hip. "Let's take a break, get something to drink."

Discussion. A change of tempo can help avoid a crisis. In this example, how might the worker's presence, understanding of the escalating activity, timing, and tone of voice influence the interaction?

Practice #2. Life Skill

Mary is sitting with six teenagers—three boys and three girls—around a table at the community center. The room is filled with books, video tapes, and snacks.

Five of the youth are working through an exercise sheet that helps them learn how to balance a checking account. One girl, Yolanda, is slouched in her chair, seemingly disinterested.

Mary rises to prepare the treat. As she fills paper cups with grapes, one of the girls says, "C'mon Yolanda."

"What for? I don't need to know how to balance no checking account. My man will give me all the money I need."

"Yeah, well, he don't even make his child support payments," another girl responds.

"Gave me this ring," Yolanda raises her hand.

"Yeah, but that don't feed your baby. You're gonna have to do that yourself, girl."

"What you laughing at?" Yolanda says to one of the boys.

"You, woman!"

Mary places a cup of grapes on the table next to the exercise sheet. The banter continues. In a few minutes Yolanda leans forward. She picks a grape from the cup, then puts her hand on the pencil.

Discussion. Sometimes the slightest gesture can make a significant difference in the outcome of an event or interaction. In this case, what did the worker do? Did her presence and capacity to interpret and understand the situation make a difference? Was her action in synch with the circumstance? How did she change the atmosphere?

Practice #3. Going to Dinner

It's getting close to dinner. The youth are in the living room of the treatment center playing table games and reading magazines. Music is playing in the background. Their worker, Angela, moves from the game table to the couch reminding them that it is almost time to begin wrapping up their activity. She leans over the back of a chair, comments on an article in a magazine, then says, "OK, let's begin to put our things away."

As she raises the overhead lights with the dimmer switch, a youth says, "Shit, I don't want to eat now. We just started this game."

"There will be time later," she responds. Slowly, she helps the youth close their magazines and box up their games.

"We're having pork chops, potatoes, beans, and apple sauce," she says.

"I can't stand pork chops," one youth says.

"Don't eat 'em then. I'll take yours," another youth responds.

They rise and she helps them tend to a few personal items. A lost shoe. A bathroom break. Then they gather near the door in a loose configuration. A sort of circle.

As they move through the door, she holds it open, then positions herself in the center of the movement as they walk down the hall to the sinks where they can wash their hands.

Discussion. Transitions are key periods in youth work. In this example, how might the worker's presence, sensitivity to meaning, and movement influence the transition from the living room to dinner? What kind of atmosphere would you want to create? How fast or slow would you move?

Practice #4. "Hanging"

Seven teenage youth are "hanging" in the hallway. They seem edgy, and the worker is worried the situation could explode if she persists in trying to get them to go outside to play ball. A couple are talking about a bad day in school. One child is staring blankly. Two others are complaining about life in general. She decides it's not time to go. It's better to just "hang" with them.

Discussion. Often a worker gets a sense that it is important to change an activity. The mood of an individual or a group is not quite right. In this example, how did the worker determine it wasn't the right time for baseball? How did her sensitivity to her own emotions help? Was it the best time to just hang? And if so, where? How did her action fit with the flow of the day?

Practice #5. Relief

Kathleen has been arguing with Troy, and the discussion is bordering on an outburst. She wants to stabilize the conversation, but can't. She is too angry herself and feels she is about to lose it. Normally, she can remain in control in these situations, but for some reason, Troy is one of those kids who can get to her.

"Matt!" she calls. "Will you please come and give me a hand. Troy and I can't seem to come to an agreement."

"Fuck you, bitch!" Troy says.

Kathleen straightens her back. "What's the problem?" Matt says, approaching.

"Well, Troy wants to play basketball, but, according to his agreement with us, he's supposed to finish his chores before he plays basketball."

"I did finish my chores, bitch," Troy says.

"I don't appreciate that kind of language," Kathleen responds, then turns to Matt. "In my opinion this floor is not swept the way it should be. There is dirt in the corners. But that's not the real issue now. We're both very upset and I think it would be best if I could take a few minutes, then come back and make sure he finishes before he plays basketball."

Matt looks at Troy and Kathleen. "Sure, I can stay here with Troy a minute."

Kathleen goes into the office a few minutes then returns determined to follow through. Later she will discuss with her colleagues why she has such a hard time with Troy. She wants to know what triggers the anger in her, so she can teach Troy to deal with his anger.

Discussion. Knowing how your feelings influence an interaction is often the key to success. Sometimes a worker has to remove herself because her emotions are interfering. In this example, was it proper for the worker to remove herself? Did she do it at the right time? How might she handle it differently next time? What would she do if no other staff were on duty?

Practice #6. Coming and Going Home

When it's time to close, the workers begin winding down some of the activities in advance, so they can say good-bye. Some youth, especially younger ones, are escorted home, but there simply are not enough escorts for the large number of youth who come to the center. As he or she leaves, each youth is invited back. "Good-bye, see you tomorrow," the worker says, as they pass through the metal detector into the night.

Discussion. Beginnings and endings are an important part of each day in youth work. In this example, what is the meaning of passing through a metal detector into the night? How might the worker's tone of voice and sense of presence help the youths?

Practice #7. Skiing

Mack, three boys, and three girls are outside cross-country skiing around a one-mile course.

With about 20 minutes and a quarter mile to go, Matt picks up the pace slightly. A couple, one boy and one girl, race ahead.

"Slow it down a little," he shouts.

Two youth in the rear seem to be struggling. He slows his pace. "Can you pick it up a little?" he asks.

"Fuck no, I hate skiing," one youth says.

"Let's watch the language," Mack says.

They finish the course within eyesight of one another and gather in the warming hut. This is the first time some of the youth have skied.

"You did pretty well," Mack says, looking at each youth. "Was it as difficult as you thought?"

"Worse," one youth says.

"Naw, cake," another responds.

"It's good for the upper body," a youth flexes his muscles.

They stand a few moments in front of the wood burner warming themselves.

Discussion. Important feelings emerge in a number of contexts. The challenge is to help youth understand these feelings as they occur. How did or didn't the worker's presence, the meaning of the activity, the movement, and the place contribute to helping you deal with feelings of frustration, inadequacy, success, etc?

Practice #8. First Visit

Ramone, a youth worker, prepares himself for the first visit with the Hills by reading the available records and reminding himself that many of the families he visits do not trust others. Like many families, the Hills have been through a series of case workers and youth workers.

Shades block the sun out of the house and a few tattered curtains cover the window in the front door. He knocks and waits a few minutes. The curtain moves slightly and he catches a glimpse of what appears to be Mrs. Hill's face. He announces who he is. The lock turns and the door slowly opens. "Hello," she says quietly. Ramone raises his hand and offers a gentle yet firm handshake.

As he steps ahead of her into the small foyer, he is filled with senses and odors. It seems as if an effort has been made to tidy the place, but the furniture is worn. The Hills' son, Robert, is leaning against the archway to the dining room. Mr. Hill in a sleeveless T-shirt is sitting in what must be his chair with a can of beer. "Want some?" he points to the can.

"No, thank you." Ramone, says.

"Please sit down," Mrs. Hill points to the couch.

"What for, we don't want his ass here," Robert says.

"You shut your...." Mr. Hill threatens before Ramone says, "I'm here, Robert, because I want to learn about what's been happening with you and your family." Then, accepting Mrs. Hill's invitation, he sits down.

Discussion. First impressions are influenced by a number of factors and often determine whether or not a successful connection and subsequent positive change will take place. How did this worker enter with sensitivity to presence, meaning, rhythm of daily life, and atmosphere?

Practice #9. Group Discussion

At least twice a day, the youth at the group home have a meeting with the workers, once in the morning before they leave for school, and once in the afternoon after they return.

One girl says, "I don't know why we have to make our beds and clean our rooms before school. The other kids in my class don't have to do this...."

"Yeah, shit, you should see how my friend keeps her room. Her mother doesn't even go in there."

Monique listens, then says, "I understand. To be honest, when I was your age my room was often a mess. But here, as you know, we are required to keep the place clean. It's important for your health, and we think it feels better to live in a place that isn't all messed up."

"What can we get from a messy room, AIDS?" one of the girls says sarcastically.

"No, of course not," Monique responds.

"I'm not saying that we want to have dirty rooms. It's just that it seems unfair for everyone to have to do it in the morning. I'd rather clean my room after school, or maybe in the evening," the girl responds. "That's the way I used to do it at home."

"Yeah, me too," another girl says.

"I can relate to that," Monique smiles. "Maybe that's an option. Why don't we discuss it together when the other workers get here?"

Discussion. Group discussions can be a vehicle for discovery and problem solving. In this example, how might the worker's presence, awareness of meanings, timing, and sensitivity to group atmosphere enhance the process?

Practice #10. Routines and Chores

"It's work, no doubt about that, but work can be fun and it feels good to accomplish something." The worker responds to a youth who has just complained about having to rake the leaves. They are working side by side in a row of workers and youth who are slowly moving together in a line across the large field surrounded by elm and oak trees. Some of the workers are singing and whistling.

"C'mon, let's get done so we can go to the park," one of the workers says. The other workers and youth begin to increase the length of their strokes, moving more quickly across the field.

Natalie walks from one room to the next helping youth make their beds and pick out clothes, being careful to do it *with* the youth but not *for* them. Although most of these youth have the skills to make their own beds and choose their own clothes, Natalie is in there, as well as in the many other moments that will continue to provide the foundation from which these youth will soon go on to live on their own. She helps them fill out job applications, make decisions, go to doctor's appointments, and open checking accounts.

As they make their beds and dress, she listens intently and shares an insight as if it is being drawn from within them and put into words by her. She remembers how frightened and excited she was when she moved out on her own.

Discussion. Routines and chores can be moments of repetitious boredom—or fulfilling learning experiences. In both of these examples, workers are trying to create a climate for the latter to occur. How does their presence and sensitivity to meaning and climate enhance their interactions with youth?

Practice #11. Confronted

"So, how old were you when you first had sex?" The girl asks her youth worker, catching the worker off guard. The worker hesitates, searches for an answer.

"You're just angry because you didn't get a big enough raise. I saw the letters come to the office. Don't be taking it out on us," a youth says to a team of somewhat disgruntled workers sitting at a dinner table.

"I'll bet you used drugs when you were a kid. You probably do even now. I saw your car at the bar on the corner with the other youth workers' cars."

Discussion. Often youth put workers on the spot. They ask a worker a question about sex or drugs to see how the worker will respond. If the worker is insincere or defensive or attempts to rationalize, they will not trust the worker, nor are they likely to be open and sincere in their responses to the worker's questions. In the above examples, how would a worker with presence respond? How would the potential meaning of the questions, the place, and timing of the responses come into play?

In the final three examples, readers are encouraged to develop their own list of questions for analyzing the situation.

Practice #12. Positioning

A group of six boys are in the game room playing Ping-Pong and pool. Four boys are playing team eight ball. Two boys are playing Ping-Pong. A worker is supervising and talking to the boys.

Two of the boys playing pool are ribbing one another in a tone that sounds like it might escalate into an argument. The worker moves closer to them.

Practice #13. Reframing

"Get out of my way, fucker, I'm leaving!" Josh says to his youth worker who is in front of the door.

"I want you to stay. It's not safe for you there," the worker says.

"I don't give a shit, I'm going," the youth steps toward the worker, then back, circling. He grabs a book, threatens to throw it, sets it down.

"Why is this so important?" the worker asks.

"Because I can't stand it here. It's better on the street."

"Why?"

"My friends are there."

The worker moves slightly away from the door, leans against the wall.

"I understand you miss your friends. But you have friends here as well."

"No, I don't. Besides, I can't do what I want here. On the street I can do whatever I want."

"Is that true?"

"Yes."

The worker waits.

"If you don't get caught," the youth smirks.

"And are the things you get caught for really the things you want?"

"Yeah, drugs, money, women. That's where it's at, man."

"And what about the cold nights and lack of food and abuse from the drug lords? Is that what you want?

"Shit, you don't know."

"No, I don't. I've never had to live like that. I only know what you've told me and what I've heard from other children."

"They don't know either. Most of them weren't there for very long. I've been out for three years, man. I know the streets."

"Tell me about it." The worker straddles a chair, leaning his chin on the backrest. The youth circles as if going for the door, then leans against the window cell across from the worker.

Practice #14. End of Day

It's dark. Three youth are sitting on a railing on the edge of the playground. A group of youth workers walk by, say goodnight. One worker pauses, sits on the railing, says, "So, what's up?"

Interactive Youth Work Curriculum

The curriculum described in this chapter is based on an outline prepared by the North American Consortium of Child and Youth Care Education Programs (NACCYCEP) [1995]. This curriculum is recommended for people who would like to teach and learn more about interactive youth work practice and is based on the following interconnected definitions and assumptions about how youth grow and develop, and how people who work with youth can be effective.

- Youth are unique, developing individuals who build and shape themselves into the world through a unique set of cultural and familial experiences [Baizerman 1993; Bruner 1990; Camino 1995; Fewster 1990; Krueger 1995; Maier 1987; Pittman 1991; Weaver 1990].

- Growth occurs in a series of moments and interactions, and each moment and interaction has enormous potential [Garfat 1995a, 1995b, 1995c; Krueger 1995; Maier 1995].

- Caring relationships and human connections are essential to healthy growth and development [Bronfenbrenner 1979; Maier 1987; NACCYCEP 1995; Zeldin et al. 1995].

67

- Competence is grounded in the capacity to be *in* the world *with* youth [Baizerman 1992; Fewster 1990].

- Competent workers choose and use methods that are geared to developmental needs [Garfat 1995a, 1995b, 1995c; Krueger 1986a, 1995; Maier 1987, 1995].

- Work with youth is a process of self in action, workers and youth learning about themselves and from their experiences together [Fewster 1990; Garfat 1995a, 1995b, 1995c; Krueger 1997a, 1997b, 1997c; Rose Sladde 1996].

- Techniques are most effective when understood and practiced in context—each situation or circumstance is unique [Areili 1996; Baizerman 1996; Krueger 1997a, 1997b, 1997c; Saleebey 1994].

- Teams of workers, groups of youth, families, and communities are interconnected systems that play key roles in youth development [Bronfenbrenner 1979; Garner 1988, 1995; Krueger 1987; Malekoff 1997; Peterson 1988, 1994; Zeldin et al. 1995].

- Work with youth requires knowledge, self-awareness, skill, compassion, commitment, energy, and the capacity to play and have fun [Krueger 1995; Waggoner 1984].

- Competent practice is continuously interlaced with other spheres of knowledge, skills, and preferred values that are learned concomitantly with the practice content [NACCYCEP 1995].

Core Content Areas

Overview of Adolescent Development

- Processes of cognitive learning and social and emotional growth [Beker & Eisikovitz 1992; Maier 1987; Redl & Wineman 1957].

- Central themes in adolescence: autonomy, identity, responsibility, moods, peer pressures, and the aches, pains, struggles and joys of being a teenager [Brendtro et al. 1990; Maier 1987; Zeldin et al. 1995].

- Youth as unique developing individuals who build and shape themselves into the world through a unique series of cultural and familial experiences [Baizerman 1993; Bruner 1990; Weaver 1990].

- Development in context: how place, tone, mood, space, and atmosphere promote growth and learning [Arieli 1996; Baizerman 1996; Freeman 1993; Garfat 1995a, 1995b, 1995c; Krueger 1997a, 1997b, 1997c; Maier 1995].

- Knowledge and examples of how each moment and interaction can serve a counseling, learning, and/or caring purpose [Krueger 1995; Maier 1987; Trieschman et al. 1969].

- An understanding of how conditions and circumstances place youth at risk [Nukkala et al. 1996].

- How anxiety, sadness, and despair influence behavior [Fewster 1990].

- The role of culture, family, and community in identity formation and skill development [Bronfenbrenner 1979; Bruner 1990; Pittman & Zeldin 1995; Weaver 1990].

- The foundations of independence: belonging, identity formation, responsibility, social skills, and connections [Brendtro et al. 1990; Pittman 1991; Pittman & Zeldin 1995].

Empowering Relationships: Core Themes, Skills, and Attitudes for Meaningful, Growth-Producing Connections and Learning Experiences

- Youth work as a process and shared journey [Baizerman 1992; Fewster 1990; Garfat 1991].

- Elements and themes in empowering interactions [Krueger 1991, 1994].

- Use of self: capacity to learn from one's experience and to understand how it influences interactions with others [Fewster 1990; Moustakas 1994; Rose Sladde 1996; Sarris 1993].

- The dynamics of relationship building: communication, reinforcement, presence, rhythmicity, expectations, acceptance, and commitment [Brendtro et al. 1990; Krueger 1997].

- Key relationship skills and ways of being: listening, empathy, being with youth in the moment [Baizerman 1993, 1995a, 1995b; Fewster 1991; Garfat 1995a, 1995b, 1995c; Krueger 1995; Maier 1987, 1995].

- Fostering an atmosphere of welcome, safety, and healthy group and individual interaction [Childress 1996; Garfat 1995a, 1995b, 1995c; Maier 1987].

Teams, Organizations, Groups, Families, and Communities as Interconnected Systems

- The ecology of teams, organizations, groups, families, and communities [Zeldin et al. 1995; Zeldin 1994].

- The developmental dynamics of groups and families [Brazeil 1996; ICYCC 1994; Malekoff 1997].

- Working within and across systems [Bronfenbrenner 1979; Zeldin et al. 1995; Peterson 1993].

- Understanding how cultural, communal, and familial experiences influence how you perceive and act in social situations [Bruner 1990; Krueger 1997a, 1997b, 1997c; Sarris 1993; Weaver 1990]

- Ingredients and conditions for effective group, team and family interactions [Brendtro et al. 1990; Garner 1988; Krueger 1987; Malekoff 1997; Maier 1987].

- Teams, groups, organizations, families, and communities as functional/ dysfunctional systems [Brendtro et al. 1990; Garner 1988; Krueger 1987; Malekoff 1997; Maier 1987].

- Family as part of who youth are [Krueger 1997a].

- Techniques of team, group, family, and community work [Brazeil 1996; Fewster 1990; Malekoff 1997; Maier 1987; Peterson 1994].

- Changing systems through healthy interaction among members of teams and organizations [Krueger 1996].

- Opportunities and sources of support for youth [Zeldin et al. 1995].

- Advocacy, networking, and collaboration [Zeldin et al. 1995; Peterson 1994].

Daily and Independent Living Skills, Job Skills, and Recreation Skills

- Recreation as a developmental, skill-building tool: understanding that each activity can play a significant role in building cognitive, social, emotional, and physical strengths [Burns 1993; Vander Ven 1995].

- Recreation and creative expression as therapy and leisure time activity [Burns 1993; Pirozak 1989; Weiser 1993].

- Learning and becoming independent as a process of learning daily living and job skills in the context of caring relationships [Garfat 1995a, 1995b, 1995c; Maier 1987].

- Skills in teaching routines, problem solving, self-care, and positive work habits [CYCLC 1988; Trieschman et al. 1969].

- Transitions as essential to successful activities and becoming independent [Krueger 1995].

Accountability: Observing, Reporting, and Outcomes

- Identifying and tracking outcomes and social competency [Zeldin et al. 1995].

- Learning how to see: making objective/subjective observations of behaviors, feelings, and skills [Garfat 1995; Krueger 1997a, 1997b, 1997c; Moustakas 1994].

- Log and report writing, articulating observations [Krueger 1986a; Trieschman et al. 1969; Walcott 1992].

- Data collection procedures: observational questioning, charting, reflective thinking [Garfat 1995; Krueger 1986a, 1986b, 1997a, 1997b, 1997c; Tireschman et al. 1969; Walcott 1992].

Discipline and Crisis Management

- Characteristics of effective discipline alternatives to punishment [Brendtro et al. 1990; Krueger 1986; Wood & Long 1991; Redl & Wineman 1957].

- Techniques of discipline [Brendtro et al. 1990; Krueger 1986a, 1986b; Wood & Long 1991; Redl & Wineman 1957].

- Understanding conflict and stress [Wood & Long 1991].

- Crises and struggles as opportunities for growth [Wood & Long 1991].

- Methods of resolving crises: counseling "on the go" [Redl & Wineman 1957; Wood & Long 1991].

Following are samples of learning outcomes and competencies for the curriculum. In preparing lesson plans and learning exercises the guide, *A Curriculum Guide for Working with Youth* [Child and Youth Care Learning Center 1998] might be helpful. This guide includes dozens of classroom exercises and resources for learning the interactive approach. The second essay in this book, "Context," provides examples for developing contextual competencies and for using a learning-centered approach in the classroom.

Learning Outcomes

- An increased awareness, understanding, and sensitivity to how youth develop.

- A greater understanding of and capacity to engage in empowering interactions.

- An understanding of and capacity to work within and across systems (teams, families, cultures, and communities).

- An enlarged repertoire of activities and techniques for engaging youth in interactions that build daily and independent living, job, and recreation skills.

- An increased ability to see and articulate significant daily interactions as separate from and part of long-term goals.

- An increased capacity (understanding and skill) to manage aggressive, antisocial, self-destructive, and/or counterproductive behavior.

Competencies

- Listening with undivided attention.

- Being dependable, predictable, and consistent.

- Placing yourself in youth's and family members' shoes and seeing the world from their cognitive, social, familial, and cultural perspectives.

- Being present, and modeling social and job skills.

- Gearing interventions (activities and techniques) to the developmental needs of children.

- Conducting an ecological assessment of a youth's family and community networks.

- Framing or reframing a situation to find mutual ground for interaction with youth from different cultural backgrounds and experiences.

- Exploring the meaning of key youth work concepts across cultures.

- Sharing personal knowledge and experiences with peers and in team meetings.

- Finding and using available opportunities and systems of support.

- Strategically planning an activity.

- Praising and encouraging youth, parents, and colleagues.

- Positively confronting youth and colleagues.

- Being consistent and following through.

- De-escalating a potential crisis situation.

- Understanding and demonstrating an ability to use discipline as a positive learning experience.

- Analyzing a behavior management problem and identifying a positive solution.

- Questioning and understanding your observations.

- Articulating interactions and patterns of developmental change.

- Identifying meaningful outcomes and processes for reaching outcomes.

- Planning and/or implementing an activity for engaging families.

- Being engaged in the activities of daily living.

- Selecting and planning a menu of activities for a week.

- Describing how a creative expressive activity can be used to help youth express themselves.

- Teaching social and independent living skills.

- Modeling independence and interdependence.

- Accessing resources and support.

Learning Methods

In addressing these assumptions, core content areas, learning outcomes and competencies, it is recommended that teachers and learners follow the learning approach discussed in the second essay, "Context."

References & Recommended Readings

Arieli, M. (1996). Do Alabama and New Moab belong to the same universe? *Child and Youth Care Forum, 25,* 289-292.

Baizerman, M. (1996). Can we get there from here: A comment on Shealy. *Child and Youth Care Forum, 25,* 285-288.

Baizerman, M. (1995a). The secret of life. *Child and Youth Care Forum, 24,* 209-210.

Baizerman, M. (1995b). Kids, place, and action(less). *Child and Youth Care Forum, 24,* 339-341.

Baizerman, M. (1993). Response: conversation by context. *Child and Youth Care Forum, 22,* 3.

Baizerman, M. (1992). Book review of "Buckets: Sketches From the Log Book of a Youth Worker" by Mark Krueger. *Child and Youth Care Forum, 21,* 129-133.

Beker, J., & Eisikovits, Z. (Eds.). (1992). *Knowledge utilization in residential child and youth care practice.* Washington DC: Child Welfare League of America.

Brazeil, D. (1996). *Family focused practice in out-of-home care.* Washington, DC: Child Welfare League of America.

Brendtro, L., Brokenleg, M., & Van Bockern, S. (1990). *Reclaiming youth at risk.* Bloomington, IN: National Education Service.

Bronfenbrenner, U. (1979). *The ecology of human development.* Cambridge, MA: Harvard University Press.

Bruner, J. (1990). *Acts of meaning.* Cambridge, MA: Harvard University Press.

Burns, M. (1993). *Time in.* Edmonton, Canada: Hignell Publications.

Camino, L. (1995). Understanding intolerance and multiculturalism: A challenge for practitioners, but also for researchers. *Journal of Adolescent Research, 10,* 155-172.

Child and Youth Care Learning Center. (1998a). *A curriculum guide for working with youth.* Milwaukee, WI: Author, University of Wisconsin-Milwaukee.

Child and Youth Care Learning Center. (1998b). *Family centered child and youth care.* Proceedings from the International Child and Youth Care Conference (ICYCC). Milwaukee, WI: Author, University of Wisconsin-Milwaukee.

Fewster, G. (1990). *Being in child care: A journey into self.* New York: Haworth.

Fewster, G. (1991). The paradoxical journey: Some thoughts on relating to children. *Journal of Child and Youth Care, 6,* v-ix.

Freeman, A. (1993). Jacob and the preacher: Conversations in context. *Child and Youth Care Forum, 22,* 245-246.

Garfat, T. (1995a). A child and youth care intervention decision. *Journal of Child and Youth Care Work, 10,* 55-61.

Garfat, T. (1995b). Editorial: Everyday life experiences for impactful child and youth care practices. *Journal of Child and Youth Care Work, 10,* v-viii.

Garfat, T. (1995c). *The effective child and youth care intervention: A phenomenological inquiry.* Doctoral dissertation, University of Victoria, British Columbia.

Garfat, T. (1991) Footprints on the borders of reality. *Journal of Child and Youth Care, 6,* 157-160.

Garner, H. (Ed.). (1995) *Teamwork models and experience in education.* Boston, MA: Allyn and Bacon.

Garner, H. (1988). *Helping others through teamwork.* Washington DC: Child Welfare League of America.

Krueger, M. A. (1997a). A contribution to the dialogue about the soul of professional development. *Child and Youth Care Forum, 20,* 411-415.

Krueger, M. A. (1997b). Learning child and youth care in context: A case example. *Journal of Child and Youth Care, 11,* 1-6.

Krueger, M. A. (1997c). Using self, story, and intuition to understand child and youth care work. *Child and Youth Care Forum, 20,* 153-161.

Krueger, M. A. (1995). *Nexus: A book about youth work.* Milwaukee, WI: Outreach Press, University of Wisconsin-Milwaukee in partnership with Child Welfare League of America.

Krueger, M. A. (1994). Framing child and youth care in moments of rhythm, presence, meaning, and atmosphere. *Child and Youth Care Forum, 23,* 223-229.

Krueger, M. A. (1991a). A review and analysis of the professional development of child and youth care work. *Child and Youth Care Forum, 20,* 379-387.

Krueger, M. A. (1991b). Coming from your center, being there, teaming up, interacting together, meeting them where they're at, counseling on the go, creating circles of care, discovering and using self, and caring for one another: Central themes in child and youth care. *Journal of Child and Youth Care, 5,* 77-87.

Krueger, M. (1987). *Floating.* Washington, DC: Child Welfare League of America.

Krueger, M. (1986a) *Intervention techniques for child and youth care workers.* Washington, DC: Child Welfare League of America.

Maier, H. (1995). Genuine child and youth care practice across the North American continent. *Journal of Child and Youth Care, 10,* 11-22.

Maier, H. (1987). *Developmental group care of children and youth.* New York: Haworth.

Malekoff, A. (1997). *Group work with adolescents: Principles and practice.* New York: Guilford Press.

Moustakas, C. (1994). *Phenomenological research methods.* Chicago: University of Chicago Press.

North American Consortium of Child and Youth Care Education Programs. (1995). Special report: Curriculum content for child and youth care practice: Recommendations of the Task Force of the North American Consortium of Child and Youth Care Education Programs. *Child and Youth Care Forum, 24,* 269-278.

Nukkala, M., Ayoub, C., Noam, G., & Selman, R. (1996). Risk and prevention: An interdisciplinary master's program in child and adolescent development. *Journal of Child and Youth Care Work, 11,* 8-32.

Peterson, R. (1994) Exploring the applications of systemic thinking in child and youth care practice: A shift in paradigm. *Journal of Child and Youth Care, 8,* 35-54.

Peterson, R. (1988). The collaborative metaphor technique: Using Ericsonian techniques and principles in child, family, and youth care work. *Journal of Child and Youth Care, 3,* 11-27.

Pirozak, E. (1989) Cards by kids: An project of art as therapy. *Journal of Child and Youth Care Work, 5,* 33-39.

Pittman, K. (1991). *A new vision: Promoting youth development.* Testimony to Congress prepared by Center for Youth Development and Policy Research, Washington, DC.

Pittman, K., & Zeldin, S. (1995). *Premises, principles, and practices: Defining the why, how, and what of promoting youth development through organizational practice.* Washington DC: Paper written for Center for Youth Development and Policy Research.

Redl, F., & Wineman, D. (1957). *Controls from within: Techniques for treatment of the aggressive child*. New York: Free Press.

Rose Sladde, L. (1996). Journal entries. *Journal of Child and Youth Care, 10,* 79-83.

Rose Sladde, L. (1991). On being a child care worker. *Journal of Child and Youth Care, 6,* 161-167.

Saleebey, D. (1994). Culture, theory, and narrative: The intersection of meanings in practice. *Social Work, 39,* 35-359.

Sarris, G. (1993). *Keeping Slug Woman alive: A holistic approach to American Indian texts*. Berkeley, CA: University of California Press.

Trieschman, A., Whittaker, J., & Brendtro, L. (1969). *The other twenty-three hours*. New York: Aldine.

Vander Ven, K. (1995). Point and level systems: Another way to fail children and youth. *Child and Youth Care Forum, 24,* 345-367.

Waggoner, C. (1984). First impressions. *Child and Youth Care Forum, 12,* 245-58.

Walcott, H. (1992) On seeking—and rejecting—validity in qualitative research. In E. Eisner & A. Peshkin (Eds.), *Qualitative inquiry in education: The continuing debate* (pp. 121-152). New York: Teachers College Press.

Weaver, G. (1990). The crisis of cross cultural child care. In M. Krueger & N. Powell (Eds.), *Choices in caring: Contemporary approaches to child and youth care work*. Washington, DC: Child Welfare League of America.

Weiser, J. (1993). *Photo therapy techniques*. San Francisco, CA: Josey Bass.

Wood, M., & Long, N. (1991). *Life space intervention*. Austin, TX: Pro-Ed.

Zeldin, S. (1994). *Stronger staff, stronger youth*. Washington DC: Center of Youth Development and Policy Research.

Zeldin, S., Tarlov, S., & Darmstadder, M. (1995). *Advancing youth development: A curriculum for youth workers*. Washington, DC: Center for Youth Development and Policy Research and National Network of Runaway and Youth Services.

Closing Thought

In discussing the will to identify—the quest to express one's uniqueness as part of a community—Vaclav Havel, the Czech playwright and president, wrote [1983, p. 301]:

> By perceiving ourselves as part of the river, we accept responsibility for the river as a whole.

In this context, work with youth is a river.

References &
Recommended Readings

Arieli, M. (1996). Do Alabama and New Moab belong to the same universe? *Child and Youth Care Forum, 25,* 289-292.

Baizerman, M. (1997). The sources of our expertise: A response to Krueger. *Child and Youth Care Forum, 26,* 417-419.

Baizerman, M. (1996). Can we get there from here: A comment on Shealy. *Child and Youth Care Forum, 25,* 285-288.

Baizerman, M. (1995a). The secret of life. *Child and Youth Care Forum, 24,* 209-210.

Baizerman, M. (1995b). Kids, place, and action(less). *Child and Youth Care Forum, 24,* 339-341.

Baizerman, M. (1993). Response: conversation by context. *Child and Youth Care Forum, 22,* 3.

Baizerman, M. (1992). Book review of "Buckets: Sketches From the Log Book of a Youth Worker" by Mark Krueger. *Child and Youth Care Forum, 21,* 129-133.

Baizerman, M., & Magnusen, D. (1996). *Vocation, calling and response as grounds to method and skill.* Paper presented at conference in residential care, Glasgow, Scotland.

Beker, J., Gittleson, P., Husted, S., Kaminstein, P., & Finkler-Adler, L. (1972). *Critical incidents in child care: A case study book.* New York: Behavioral Publications.

Beker, J., & Eisikovits, Z. (Eds.). (1992). *Knowledge utilization in residential child and youth care practice.* Washington DC: Child Welfare League of America.

Benning, S. (1994). *Videos by Sadie Benning.* Chicago: Video data bank.

Brazeil, D. (1996). *Family focused practice in out-of-home care.* Washington, DC: Child Welfare League of America.

Brendtro, L., Brokenleg, M., & Van Bockern, S. (1990). *Reclaiming youth at risk.* Bloomington, IN: National Education Service.

Bronfenbrenner, U. (1979). *The ecology of human development.* Cambridge, MA: Harvard University Press.

Bruner, J. (1990). *Acts of meaning.* Cambridge, MA: Harvard University Press.

Burns, M. (1993). *Time in.* Edmonton, Canada: Hignell Publications.

Camino, L. (1995). Understanding intolerance and multiculturalism: A challenge for practitioners, but also for researchers. *Journal of Adolescent Research, 10,* 155-172.

Child and Youth Care Learning Center. (1998). *A curriculum guide for working with youth.* Milwaukee, WI: Author, University of Wisconsin-Milwaukee.

Child and Youth Care Learning Center. (1998). *Leavin' and livin': New days, new ways.* Milwaukee, WI: Author, University of Wisconsin-Milwaukee.

Child and Youth Care Learning Center. (1998). *Family centered child and youth care.* Proceedings from the International Child and Youth Care Conference (ICYCC). Milwaukee, WI: Author, University of Wisconsin-Milwaukee.

Childress, H. (1996). *Landscapes of betrayal; landscapes of joy: Curtisville in the lives of its teenagers.* Doctoral dissertation, University of Wisconsin-Milwaukee.

Craig, E. (1978). The heart of the teacher: A heuristic study of the inner world of teaching. *Dissertation Abstracts International, 38,* 7222A.

Csikszentmihalyi, M. (1990). *Flow: The psychology of optimal experience.* New York: Harper and Row.

Desjardins, S., & Freeman, A. (1991). Out of sync. *Journal of Child and Youth Care, 6,* 139-144.

Fahlberg, V. (1990). *Residential treatment: A tapestry of many therapies.* Indianapolis, IN: Perspectives Press.

Fewster, G. (1990). *Being in child care: A journey into self.* New York: Haworth.

Fewster, G. (1991a). The paradoxical journey: Some thoughts on relating to children. *Journal of Child and Youth Care, 6,* v-ix.

Fewster, G. (1991b). The third person singular: Writing about the child care relationship. *Journal of Child and Youth Care Work, 7,* 55-62.

Freeman, A. (1993). Jacob and the preacher: Conversations in context. *Child and Youth Care Forum, 22,* 245-246.

Garfat, T. (1995a). A child and youth care intervention decision. *Journal of Child and Youth Care Work, 10,* 55-61.

Garfat, T. (1995b). Editorial: Everyday life experiences for impactful child and youth care practices. *Journal of Child and Youth Care Work, 10,* v-viii.

Garfat, T. (1995c). *The effective child and youth care intervention: A phenomenological inquiry.* Doctoral dissertation, University of Victoria, British Columbia.

Garfat, T. (1991) Footprints on the borders of reality. *Journal of Child and Youth Care, 6,* 157-160.

Garner, H. (Ed.). (1995) *Teamwork models and experience in education.* Boston, MA: Allyn and Bacon.

Garner, H. (1988). *Helping others through teamwork.* Washington DC: Child Welfare League of America.

Glasser, G., & Strauss, A. (1967). *The discovery of grounded theory.* Chicago: Aldine.

Gleick, J. (1987). *Chaos: Making a new science.* New York: Viking.

Goffman, I. (1959). *The presentation of self in everyday life.* New York: Doubleday.

Hall, E. (1976). *Beyond culture.* Garden City, NY: Anchor Books.

Havel, V. (1983). *Letters to Olga.* New York: Henry Holt & Company.

Husserl, E. (1970). *Logical investigations.* New York: Humanities Press.

Inner City Youth Serving Agencies. (1996). *Social competency inventory.* Milwaukee, WI: Child and Youth Care Learning Center.

Jacobs, H. (1995). The direct care practice concentration: A new development in the education of direct care practitioners. *Journal of Child and Youth Care Work, 10,* 37-53.

Krueger, M. A. (1997a). A contribution to the dialogue about the soul of professional development. *Child and Youth Care Forum, 20,* 411-415.

Krueger, M. A. (1997b). Learning child and youth care in context: A case example. *Journal of Child and Youth Care, 11,* 1-6.

Krueger, M. A. (1997c). Using self, story, and intuition to understand child and youth care work. *Child and Youth Care Forum, 20,* 153-161.

Krueger, M. A. (1995). *Nexus: A book about youth work.* Milwaukee, WI: Outreach Press, University of Wisconsin-Milwaukee in partnership with Child Welfare League of America.

Krueger, M. A. (1994). Framing child and youth care in moments of rhythm, presence, meaning, and atmosphere. *Child and Youth Care Forum, 23,* 223-229.

Krueger, M. A. (1991a). A review and analysis of the professional development of child and youth care work. *Child and Youth Care Forum, 20,* 379-387.

Krueger, M. A. (1991b). Coming from your center, being there, teaming up, interacting together, meeting them where they're at, counseling on the go, creating circles of care, discovering and using self, and caring for one another: Central themes in child and youth care. *Journal of Child and Youth Care, 5,* 77-87.

Krueger, M. (1987). *Floating.* Washington, DC: Child Welfare League of America.

Krueger, M. (1986a) *Intervention techniques for child and youth care workers.* Washington, DC: Child Welfare League of America.

Krueger, M. (1986b). *Job satisfaction for child and youth care workers.* Washington, DC: Child Welfare League of America.

Maier, H. (1995). Genuine child and youth care practice across the North American continent. *Journal of Child and Youth Care, 10,* 11-22.

Maier, H. (1994). A therapeutic environmental approach. *Research and Evaluation, 3*, 3-4.

Maier, H. (1992). Rhythmicity: A powerful force for experiencing unity and personal connections. *Journal of Child and Youth Care Work, 8*, 7-13.

Maier, H. (1989). Role playing: Structures and educational objectives. *Journal of Child and Youth Care, 4*, 41-37.

Maier, H. (1987). *Developmental group care of children and youth.* New York: Haworth.

Malekoff, A. (1997). *Group work with adolescents: Principles and practice.* New York: Guilford Press.

McElroy, J. (1991). Letter to Rick Small. *Journal of Child and Youth Care Work, 7*, 36.

Moustakas, C. (1994). *Phenomenological research methods.* Chicago: University of Chicago Press.

Nabokov, P. (1981). *Indian running: Native American history and tradition.* Santa Fe, NM: Ancient City Press.

North American Consortium of Child and Youth Care Education Programs. (1995). Special report: Curriculum content for child and youth care practice: Recommendations of the Task Force of the North American Consortium of Child and Youth Care Education Programs. *Child and Youth Care Forum, 24*, 269-278.

Nguyen, P. (1992). Journal at the shelter. *Child and Youth Care Forum, 21*, 92-104.

Nukkala, M., Ayoub, C., Noam, G., & Selman, R. (1996). Risk and prevention: An interdisciplinary master's program in child and adolescent development. *Journal of Child and Youth Care Work, 11*, 8-32.

Ortiz, S. (1992). *Woven stone.* Phoenix, AZ: University of Arizona Press.

Peterson, R. (1994) Exploring the applications of systemic thinking in child and youth care practice: A shift in paradigm. *Journal of Child and Youth Care, 8*, 35-54.

Peterson, R. (1994) The adrenaline metaphor: Narrative mind and practice in child and child and youth care. *Journal of Child and Youth Care, 9*, 107-122.

Peterson, R. (1988). The collaborative metaphor technique: Using Ericsonian techniques and principles in child, family, and youth care work. *Journal of Child and Youth Care, 3*, 11-27.

Pirozak, E. (1989) Cards by kids: An project of art as therapy. *Journal of Child and Youth Care Work, 5*, 33-39.

Pittman, K. (1991). *A new vision: Promoting youth development.* Testimony to Congress prepared by Center for Youth Development and Policy Research, Washington, DC.

Pittman, K., & Zeldin, S. (1994). *From deterrence to development: Putting programs for young African American males in perspective.* Washington DC: The Urban Institute.

Pittman, K., & Zeldin, S. (1995). *Premises, principles, and practices: Defining the why, how, and what of promoting youth development through organizational practice.* Washington DC: Paper written for Center for Youth Development and Policy Research.

Polyani, M. (1969). *Knowing and being.* (Majorie Greene, Ed.). Chicago: University of Chicago Press.

Polyani, M. (1983) *The tacit dimension.* Garden City, NY: Doubleday.

Rapoport, 1990. *The meaning of built environment: A non-verbal communication approach.* Phoenix, AZ: University of Arizona Press.

Redl, F. (1959). Strategy and technique of the Life-Space Interview. *American Journal of Orthopsychiatry, 29,* 1-18.

Redl, F., & Wineman, D. (1957). *Controls from within: Techniques for treatment of the aggressive child.* New York: Free Press.

Richmond, P. (1998). Untitled paper on boundaries. University of Wisconsin-Milwaukee.

Rose Sladde, L. (1996). Journal entries. *Journal of Child and Youth Care, 10,* 79-83.

Rose Sladde, L. (1991). On being a child care worker. *Journal of Child and Youth Care, 6,* 161-167.

Saleebey, D. (1994). Culture, theory, and narrative: The intersection of meanings in practice. *Social Work, 39,* 35-359.

Sarris, G. (1993). *Keeping Slug Woman alive: A holistic approach to American Indian texts.* Berkeley, CA: University of California Press.

Tausig, H. (1992). Tasha. *The Journal of Child and Youth Care Work, 8,* 54-58.

Trieschman, A., Whittaker, J., & Brendtro, L. (1969). *The other twenty-three hours.* New York: Aldine.

Vander Ven, K. (1988). Book review. "Chaos: Making a New Science" by James Gleick. *The Child and Youth Care Administrator, 1,* 71-72.

Vander Ven, K. (1995). Point and level systems: Another way to fail children and youth. *Child and Youth Care Forum, 24,* 345-367.

Vander Ven, K., Mattingly, M., & Morris, M. (1982). Principles and guidelines for child care preparation programs. *Child Care Quarterly, 11,* 221-244.

Vygotsky, L. S. (1978) *Mind in society.* Cambridge, MA: Harvard University Press.

Waggoner, C. (1984). First impressions. *Child and Youth Care Forum, 12,* 245-58.

Walcott, H. (1992) On seeking—and rejecting—validity in qualitative research. In E. Eisner & A. Peshkin (Eds.), *Qualitative inquiry in education: The continuing debate* (pp. 121-152). New York: Teachers College Press.

Weaver, G. (1990). The crisis of cross cultural child care. In M. Krueger & N. Powell (Eds.), *Choices in caring: Contemporary approaches to child and youth care work.* Washington, DC: Child Welfare League of America.

Weiser, J. (1993). *Photo therapy techniques.* San Francisco, CA: Josey Bass.

Williams, P. (1995). *Developing a model to ease youth's transition into residential treatment.* Practicum, NOVA/Southeastern University.

Wood, M., & Long, N. (1991). *Life space intervention.* Austin, TX: Pro-Ed.

Zeldin, S. (1994). *Stronger staff, stronger youth.* Washington DC: Center of Youth Development and Policy Research.

Zeldin, S., Tarlov, S., & Darmstadder, M. (1995). *Advancing youth development: A curriculum for youth workers.* Washington, DC: Center for Youth Development and Policy Research and National Network of Runaway and Youth Services.

Resources

The following authors, books, articles, and videos have had a significant impact on my thinking about youth work. Full references for each of the books and articles can be found in "References & Recommended Readings."

Mike Baizerman writes an ongoing column, "Musing with Mike," in *Child and Youth Care Forum*, in which he explores youth work as a lived experience. His writing provides thought-provoking ideas about youth work as a vocation and a way of being with youth. I find him to be one of the most stimulating writers in the field. He blends his gut-level awareness of the work with theoretical, philosophical, and spiritual ideas that make me return to his columns again and again.

Jerome Beker is Editor of *Child and Youth Care Forum*. In addition to editing the oldest and most comprehensive documentation of the development of our field, his own editorial columns, articles, and books have been significant contributions to this literature. From his book, *Knowledge Utilization in Residential Child and Youth Care Practice*, to his early pioneering work, *Critical Incidents in Child and Youth Care*, he has been a leader and mentor in challenging the field to pursue new directions in developing a profession.

Sadie Benning developed a powerful, prize-winning video as she traveled through her adolescence. *Videos by Sadie Benning* is available from the Video Data Bank at the Chicago Institute of Art. The sexual, emotional, and social challenges and paradoxes of being a youth are vividly portrayed in scenes from her room and neighborhood. An excellent series for classroom teaching and for getting back in touch with what it means to be a teenager.

Jerome Bruner's thought-provoking book, *Acts of Meaning*, explores how humans build and shape themselves into the world through unique cognitive experiences. This work provides excellent insight for understanding how youth make meaning within different cultural contexts and how they interpret reality based on the evolving cognitive narratives that they carry in their minds.

"Out of Sync," an article by **Sylviane Desjardins** and **A. Freeman** that appeared in the *Journal of Child and Youth Care*, is an excellent example of the stories that are now being told in youth work journals. The authors provide a real example of a day in a group home. You can feel and see the rhythms of daily living as workers struggle and succeed.

Gary Fewster is a founding editor of the *Journal of Child and Youth Care*, a journal with stories, research, art, program descriptions, and editorials that portray child and youth care as it is and reads like it feels. Fewster's editorials and articles richly explore youth work as a process of self in action and self-discovery. In his classic novel, *Being in Child Care: A Journal into Self*, he shows how an understanding of one's experiences leads to understanding children and youth. The novel is based on a female supervisor's conversation with a male worker about many of the sexual and emotional issues that workers encounter in their interactions with children and youth. Fewster is a true original who throughout his career has challenged members of the field to stay focused on use of self in relationships. Fewster walks the talk. And he has a great sense of humor.

Everything **Henry Maier** has written is a valuable addition to the youth work scholar's and practitioner's knowledge base. Perhaps more than any other writer in the field, he has provided the field with useful and thoughtful examples of how developmental principles, concepts, and techniques are integrated into relationships with children. If you haven't read his work, a good place to begin is with the classic, *Developmental Group Care of Children and Youth*. Then move to articles such as **"Genuine Child and Youth Care Practice Across the North American Continent"** and **"Rhythmicity: A Powerful Force for Experiencing Unity and Personal Connections."** Maier led the task group of the North American Consortium of Child and Youth Care Programs that developed the curriculum that was the foundation for the curriculum in the final chapter of this book. He was largely responsible for NACCYCEP curriculum's interpersonal/interactive/contextual flavor. Like many others, I consider him to be a mentor. Throughout the writing of this book, he provided helpful insights.

Along with Gerry Fewster, **Thom Garfat** is Editor of *Journal of Child and Youth Care*. His writings about relationships, child and youth care interventions, and self-awareness have been instrumental in developing a knowledge base for the field that is rooted in context and meaning. His award-winning dissertation, **"The Effective Child and Youth Care Intervention: A Phenomenological Inquiry,"** examines the meaning of child and youth care intervention. This is a front-running piece of research that has been instrumental in shaping the qualitative, interpersonal, contextual direction that seems to ring true with the way many members of the field experience youth work. Throughout his career, Thom has successfully blended creativity, experience, and objectivity into his work. I have often been moved by his writings.

Karen Vander Ven is the most prolific writer in the field. Her work ranges from recreational activities to models of professional development. She is also a leader in the movement toward lifespan care and development. Equally comfortable in speaking about early childhood, youth work, and work with the elderly, throughout her career, she has pushed the field to think in new ways and offered theoretically sound and practice-based examples of daily work with others. Karen is also Editor of *Journal of Child and Youth Care Work*, a journal that focuses on practice-based contributions from direct line workers and teachers of youth work practice. If you haven't read Karen's work, her column in the journal and her recent *Point and Level Systems: Another Way to Fail Children and Youth* are good places to begin. Karen can often be found playing basketball at child and youth care conferences. She's always open to a game of one on one.

About the Author

Mark A. Krueger, Ph.D., is Professor and Director of the Child and Youth Care Learning Center at the University of Wisconsin-Milwaukee. He has taught youth work for 20 years. Prior to coming to the university, he was a youth worker for 11 years. His books include *Intervention Techniques for Child/Youth Care Workers, Job Satisfaction for Child and Youth Care Workers, Careless to Caring for Troubled Youth,* and *Nexus: A Book about Youth Work.* He has also written two novels about youth work, *Floating* and *In Motion,* and a book of short stories, *Buckets: Sketches from a Youth Worker's Log Book.* Dr. Krueger has contributed several stories and articles to journals, including *Child Welfare.* Throughout his career, he has been an active member of the effort to develop the profession of child and youth care work.

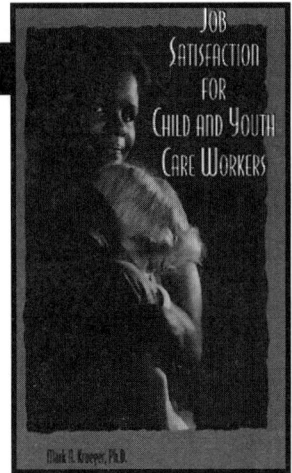

Job Satisfaction for Child and Youth Care Workers (Third Edition)
Mark A. Krueger

Job satisfaction may be defined in several ways. It is a feeling of fulfillment associated with working. It is also an attitude about various facets of a job, such as working conditions, supervision, and decisionmaking. Job satisfaction in child and youth care is crucial because at-risk children and families need competent, enthusiastic workers who can be depended upon. In this third edition, the premise is that job satisfaction comes from many personal sources and is nourished by supportive agency practices, daily interactions, and long-term goals.

To Order: 1996/0-87868-604-5   Stock #6045 $14.95

Write:	CWLA c/o PMDS	Call: 800/407-6273
	P.O. Box 2019	301/617-7825
	Annapolis Junction, MD 20701	
e-mail:	cwla@pmds.com	Fax: 301/206-9789

Please specify stock #6045. Bulk discount policy (not for resale): 10-49 copies 10%, 50-99 copies 20%, 100 or more copies 40%. Canadian and foreign orders must be prepaid in U.S. funds. MasterCard/Visa accepted.

Price Reduced!

Nexus: A Book About Youth Work
Mark A. Krueger

Published by Outreach Press
in partnership with CWLA Press

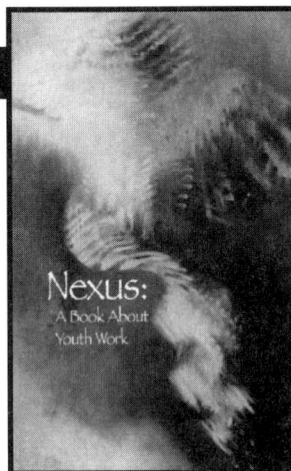

This book demonstrates the techniques for

forming relationships and empowering at-risk youth to grow. Its

unique case study/story format showcases the elements that form

empowering communications and demonstrates how behavior

management, social learning, daily living, and recreation tech-

niques and practices are effectively implemented in transitions,

activities, and crises.

To Order: 1995/0-9646955-0-2   Stock #6347 $5.50

Write: CWLA c/o PMDS   Call: 800/407-6273
         P.O. Box 2019   301/617-7825
         Annapolis Junction, MD 20701
e-mail: cwla@pmds.com   Fax: 301/206-9789

Please specify stock #6347. Bulk discount policy (not for resale): 10-49 copies 10%,
50-99 copies 20%, 100 or more copies 40%. Canadian and foreign orders must be
prepaid in U.S. funds. MasterCard/Visa accepted.

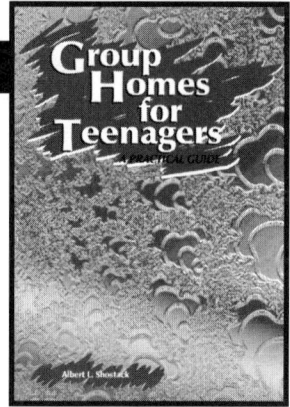

Group Homes for Teenagers:
A Practical Guide
Albert L. Shostack

A detailed "toolkit" for starting and running a
community-based group home, *Group Homes for Teenagers* offers a
holistic and integrated approach to group care service. It takes into
account the needs of the individual, the family, and the surrounding social environment within the context of available community
and government resources. A must for group home operators and
staff members, caseworkers, and all others concerned with quality
group care service delivery!

To Order: 1997/0-87868-691-6   Stock #6916 $16.95

Write:	CWLA c/o PMDS	Call: 800/407-6273
	P.O. Box 2019	301/617-7825
	Annapolis Junction, MD 20701	
e-mail:	cwla@pmds.com	Fax: 301/206-9789

Please specify stock #6916. Bulk discount policy (not for resale): 10-49 copies 10%,
50-99 copies 20%, 100 or more copies 40%. Canadian and foreign orders must be
prepaid in U.S. funds. MasterCard/Visa accepted.